OLD DANISH SILVER

GUDMUND BOESEN AND CHR. A. BØJE

OLD DANISH SILVER

HASSING PUBLISHER

COPENHAGEN MCMXLIX

TRANSLATED BY RONALD KAY
LAY-OUT BY PETER KOCH
PRINTED BY H. P. HANSENS BOGTRYKKERI
COPENHAGEN
DENMARK

CONTENTS

PREFACE

INTRODUCTION

Use of silver at table, its form and decoration

by

Gudmund Boesen

Goldsmiths and their technique

by

Chr. A. Bøje

INDEX

of marks and owners, and bibliography

Lists of Goldsmiths

ILLUSTRATIONS

This book is a translation of a work which is appearing simultaneously in Danish as the first of a series of richly illustrated books on the applied arts in Denmark in past ages, to be published in Copenhagen by the firm of Alfred G. Hassing. This series will deal mainly with the history of the domestic arts, and so the present volume on Danish silver only treats of silver used in the service of food and drink. Even though such things as ecclesiastical plate, articles of the toilet etc. are thereby excluded, silver used at table has nevertheless always formed the most comprehensive part of the goldsmith's output, and this book should therefore give a fairly complete impression of the most important aspects of the Danish goldsmith's art from about 1550 to 1840.

Larger works on old Danish silver are two volumes of fundamental importance written in Danish by Jørgen Olrik (1909 and 1915). But the present book is the first on this subject to appear in a world language.

In the first section of the introduction Gudmund Boesen deals with some aspects of the use of domestic silver and its style and decoration, while Chr. A. Bøje discusses the technique of the goldsmiths' craft and the conditions under which they worked in Denmark. The main part of the book consists of photographs, arranged so far as possible in chronological order, so that the development of each type of article may be traced.

We are grateful for the kindness and help we have received from many quarters in the preparation of this book. His Majesty the King of Denmark has given permission for the reproduction of various articles belonging to the Royal Household Silver. Museums in Denmark and abroad have lent us pictures. Many of their officials have helped us in various ways; and we have also received support from the staff of Danish libraries and archives. A large number of private owners have with extraordinary kindness opened their homes to us and readily put their collections at our disposal to study and to photograph. Without all this support our work could not have been performed.

And finally, thanks are due to Mr. Ronald Kay for his careful and sympathetic translation and to Mr. Charles Oman for his courtesy in giving us the benefit of his unrivalled knowledge.

Gudmund Boesen.   *Chr. A. Bøje.*

Feast given by King Frederik III at Frederiksborg Castle in 1658 in honour of King Karl Gustav of Sweden. Part of an engraving in *Pufendorf: Res gestae Caroli Gustavi*. In front at the head of the table sits the Danish Queen, on her right the Swedish king and then Frederik III. On his right stands the carver in the act of carving a joint with carving-knife and fork. In the table are three show-dishes, the middle one a peacock; as for silver, only plates and dishes are to be seen. From the door in the background the next course is being brought in (see p. 18). On the right of the door is a dresser with a display of goblets and other gold- and silverware; in front of it a page is bending over a slop-basin or a wine-cooler on the floor.

Even as far back as the early Middle Ages men of great conse-quence in Denmark owned a certain number of gold and silver bowls and drinking vessels, but only in exceptional cases have such mediaeval articles been preserved. When the Renaissance, ac-companied by the Lutheran Reformation, spread to Denmark there was a great increase in the use of the precious metals in the manu-facture of plate and jewellery. This was bound up with the Re-naissance love of splendid display, but had as a background two factors: first, the increased wealth in Denmark resulting from the rise in prices of Danish agricultural produce, and secondly, the stream of silver that in the middle of the 16th Century began to flow to Europe from the silver mines in the newly-discovered continent of America. The great demand for articles of gold and silver —es-pecially the latter— laid the foundation for the development of the goldsmith's craft in Denmark (where in the Middle Ages goldsmiths had been few in number). At the same time the increased production of silverware has naturally resulted in more articles being preserved to-day. And so through them it becomes possible to give an impres-sion of the development of Danish silverware from about the middle of the 16th Century.

There was a great deal of intemperate drinking throughout the 16th and the greater part of the 17th Centuries. Among all classes of society it was an everyday occurrence to drink oneself senseless. Even at the end of the 17th Century a French Ambassador could speak with dismay of the tremendous flagons he had had to drain at a festivity held by Ulrik Frederik Gyldenløve, the half-brother of the king, a man whom foreign visitors used to regard as one of the most highly cultivated Danes at that time. Whether the drink con-sisted of beer or home-produced fruit wine ("most", already popular in the 16th Century) —whether it was brandy or, as became custo-mary among the upper classes, imported French, Spanish or Rhenish wines,— people could of course drink from the cheap old-fashioned wooden tankards or beakers or from the tin tankards which became more and more common from the 16th Century onwards. But it lent special lustre both to the host and to the occasion if the drink could be served from vessels of gold and silver. In the houses of the rich all the cups of precious metal were put out on a special sideboard on festive occasions. As time went on it became customary to drink from glasses, but certain toasts were still drunk from big silver tankards. Usually the tankard went round from mouth to mouth and everyone took a considerable pull. Very often Danish tankards are marked on the inside with small silver pegs; everyone had to drink exactly from one peg to the next. The word "peg" in Danish ("pæl") soon came to indicate a definite volume and the size of Danish tankards was referred to by specifying their contents in "pegs" or "pots" (1 pot = 4 pegs).

Not until the early 18th Century did silver drinking cups go out of general use; and thereafter they continued to be made for ornamental purposes, often as gifts (as with christening cups and sports trophies in our own day).

From a catalogue of Christian II's silver dating from 1523 it may be seen that the King then owned more than 50 cups, tankards, etc. — the heaviest cups had a weight of about 5 kgs. But the numbers involved became much greater by the end of the 16th Century. Noble, bourgeois and even peasant followed suit, as his purse allowed. By the end of the century it was the usual thing in a peasant's home to find at least one silver cup. In the surviving catalogues of the household silver in the possession of the King and the nobility may be seen the names of many different types of drinking cup. The most common were tankards of varying size with handle and hinged lid. Originally these were containers from which the wine was decanted, but in Renaissance times it was customary to drink direct from the tankard. Two types survived from the Middle Ages: one cylindrical, the other with swelling sides and tapering neck. The latter must certainly have been the less common; sometimes there was a spout. Only a single example of a cup of this type designed for secular use has been preserved. It was part of Frederik II's household silver (No. 97).

This was presumably used as a wine decanter; in a letter of 1639, moreover, Christian IV mentions a gold water jug, on which must be set »a crooked beak like that on all common water jugs« — this was certainly the same type. But much more popular was the cylindrical tankard; it was well adapted for drinking and retained its popularity as long as tankards were made for this purpose. In the Renaissance this type was quite tall and slender, with a moulded base. Often a ring encircled the lower part of the tankard, thus forming a kind of plinth above the base. Towards the middle of the 17th Century tankards became lower as a rule; soon the rim base disappeared, and there emerged the Baroque type, strong, low and broad, resting on three feet which were usually in the form of pomegranates

Silver treasure (Danish National Museum). The most valued possessions of a well-to-do peasant: tankard, Rummer beaker and six spoons of different types, all silver, buried to escape plundering during the Swedish war in the middle of the 17th Century and not discovered until the present day.

or lions sejant. In general, this form remained through the succeeding ages. In the Renaissance the thumb-piece on the lid was often flat and cast in relief; when feet were added to the tankard the thumb-piece was usually made to match; a tankard with pomegranate feet would have a double thumb-piece with two smaller pomegranates.

Along with the tankards there are also references to »skovere«, which seem to have been very large drinking vessels, and »stobe«. Possibly these names refer to different types of goblet, with a high foot and with or without lid. Goblets were popular during the Renaissance but less common afterwards, except for ceremonial use: they are for instance found among church and gild silver, which has always been more conservative in its design. The only examples of the goblet form being retained for popular use are the small brandy or schnapps goblets; here the form persisted until well on in the 19th Century.

The most common of all drinking vessels were beakers without foot; they were usually round, but sometimes also —especially during the Renaissance— polygonal. They were to be found in various sizes and could at times hold as much as a litre. A type very common at the end of the 16th and beginning of the 17th Centuries had a spreading rim and moulded base; usually a twisted rope adorned with cherub heads surrounded the lower part of the beaker. This type of beaker continued in use in a degenerate form until the 18th Century. Other more simple cylindrical types of beaker, usually narrowing slightly at the bottom, were to be found alongside the "cherub" beakers and as time went on became more popular. Towards the end of the 17th Century some of these beakers, like the tankards, acquired feet in the form of pomegranates, balls etc. Curved types of beaker were made in the Rococo period. Sometimes the beakers had lids, but most often not.

A special variety of beaker was the "Silver Rummer" (sølvrømer) which appeared often during the Renaissance. It is reminiscent of the Rummer Glass and has a low cylindrical gadrooned foot below the barrel- or bowl-shaped beaker. Finally mention must be made of the more bizarre shapes of drinking vessels that were also popular during the Renaissance, cups shaped like animals, human beings or various objects. Reference is often made to "virgin beakers" or "mill beakers"; an example of the latter, of somewhat later date, may be found in the Danish National Museum (illustrated here as No. 85).

The tumbler dates from the Baroque period onwards. This was a small, hemi-spherical beaker whose centre of gravity was so arranged that it always righted itself when placed on its side (cf. text to No. 87). Also used as drinking vessel during the Renaissance was a low bowl with flat lug handle ("kovsken" — cf. No. 309).

During the first half of the 18th Century there occurred a complete revolution in drinking habits in Denmark. It became fashionable to drink wine from a glass, and beer declined in status and became the drink of the common people. Even "øllebrød", a dish made of bread soaked in beer, which had been the standard breakfast dish of the previous centuries, disappeared from the breakfast table of cultivated people and was replaced by the drinks of a newer age. Coffee, tea and chocolate were drunk in Denmark from the 1660's at least. In 1665 the doctor and botanist Simon Paulli could write a dissertation on the misuse of tobacco and tea. In 1669 Anders Bording writes in his rhyming newspaper "The Danish Mercury" some lines which may be freely translated as follows:

"Then first to northern lands and climes there came
Such rare and pleasant drinks of various name
Chocolate, and tea, and coffee they were called . . ."

In 1672 mention is made in Count Griffenfeldt's housekeeping books of the purchase of coffee cups and pots; from 1691 onwards there are frequent references to tea-, chocolate- and coffee-houses in Copenhagen in addition to wine- and ale-houses. It appears from inventories of about 1700 that articles used in the service of tea and coffee were generally to be found in a well-to-do-household at that time. A Court Journal of the same years reveals that at that time the king drank either tea, coffee or chocolate every morning, and in 1697 Bishop Jens Bircherod relates in his diary that on the morning of 17th November he visited his Minister, Baron Jens Juel, and sat for an hour drinking tea and discussing business with him.

The new drinks were generally taken in porcelain cups and pots, and the bowls to match were also of porcelain. But silver was used also. The oldest existing silver coffee-pots (dating from 1717 and the years immediately following, see No. 100 et seq.) inherited the design of the wine jug but usually had an insulating wooden handle. The tea-pots on the other hand borrowed their form from Chinese porcelain.

While coffee-pots often had feet, this was not so with tea-pots in the early 18th Century. These had practically always a dish to match, which only partially succeeded in insulating the hot tea-pot when it was placed on the table (the coffee-pots without feet had a similar accessory). And so later in the century tea-pots as well as coffee-pots were made with feet. Among the Royal Household Silver is a tea-pot with the Copenhagen hall-mark 1708, but as it has been altered in the 1730's there is some doubt whether this was ever a tea-pot originally; the oldest silver tea-pot surviving is thought to date from the 1720's. But even in 1719 a prosperous Copenhagen citizen could leave behind in his will a coffee- and a tea-pot, both of silver.

In the later 18th Century the expression "tea-service" may be met with in inventories. This comprises a number of articles which formed part of a well-furnished tea- or coffee-table: as a rule two tea-pots, (usually one bigger than the other), a coffee-pot and a milk-jug, two tea canisters, a tea urn, one or two slop-basins, a sugar box or two sugar bowls or dishes, and sometimes six or a dozen tea-spoons. When such a service was first produced as a complete unit is not certain. Among the Royal Household Silver is a service of homogeneous design, fluted and engraved with Queen Sophie Magdalene's monogram, but it was made by more than one goldsmith and over a period from 1738 to 1745 —and the tea canisters even as early as 1724. In 1761 an old service consisting of the same pieces was sent to be melted down, as being already antiquated in form. From the middle of the century the same articles are mentioned in inventories and are listed in such a way that they seem to have belonged together. In a manor-house in Fyn may still be seen parts of what was evidently a bigger service dating from ca. 1749 (illustrated as No. 108) and more complete services are known to date from the 1760's. But it was much more common for people to have odd pieces only made of silver.

Coffee was originally drunk with warm milk; as a rule milk-jugs seem to have had the same form as coffee-jugs, and like these, often had a dish to match in the first half of the century. Only after the middle of the century is there mention of cream bowls (or milk bowls) and cream ladles (milk ladles); about 1770 milk jugs seem to disappear. In Copenhagen porcelain sets dating from the 1780's is usually found a small cream jug; this was also made in silver, but it is not clear whether cream jugs of this kind can have been in use about the middle of the century (cf. No. 154, which is most likely a cream jug). Possibly some of the small sauce-boats (e. g. No. 359) were used for cream.

Throughout the 18th Century occur references to silver tea-kettles. Some of these have survived, usually along with a warming-dish. But urns were much more popular for holding the hot water with which to make tea; if made of silver they belonged to the show-pieces of a fashionable home. Sometimes tea-urns were used only as containers for water, which had first to be heated, but the proper tea-urns were fitted with a firing arrangement using wood fuel; the smoke outlet was led like a chimney up through the inside. Sometimes a spirit lamp was used instead of wood fuel. The water was drawn off through a tap. One of Christian IV's letters dated 1639 mentions a gold water jug with tap, and in the same way water was tapped from the big water fountains which were to be seen in the 18th Century dining-room; these also were sometimes made of silver. In Rosenborg Castle is a conical Chinese porcelain jug with Danish silver mounting from the period 1700—1730; this also has a tap and was probably a hot water container for use in making tea. The oldest surviving silver tea-urn dates from 1733; this too is conical. But the other older tea urns known still to exist are bulbous in shape, and in the rococo period

Gold tea-service, made by Thomas Andreas Westrup, Copenhagen 1761—62 for Count
A. G. Moltke—now at Rosenborg Castle. In front are two tea-pots and two sugar-boxes,
behind are a coffee-pot, two tea-canisters, a slop-basin and a milk jug.

were closely related in design to the contemporary coffee-pot with
legs. During the neo-classical period the tea urn naturally took on
a vase form, and spherical urns were often to be seen in the Empire
period.

Along with the tea urn there were always one, or more often two
slop-basins for use when rinsing tea-pots or cups with hot water from
the urn. Slop-basins are mentioned as early as 1700.

An indispensable part of the tea-service was the tea-canister. According to accounts relating to the beginning of the 18th Century
there were as a general rule two kinds of tea on sale: green tea and
Bohe tea (referred to in Holberg's "Barselstuen" in 1724 as "Thee de
Bou"). As a rule there were two tea-canisters to match, or canisters
with two compartments. A single canister of this type with two compartments (No. 183) has engraved on the lid a G and a B, the initials
of the two types of tea. Tea canisters have a wide diversity of form.
The oldest one extant dates from 1701 and has a simple box form
with rectangular sides and flat lid. More common, however, is a
canister with a small domed cap; octagonal, oval and cylindrical types
are all met with. In the Rococo period the tea canisters assumed the
then fashionable pear shape, reminiscent of the contemporary sugar-
casters, and later followed vase-shaped and barrel-shaped canisters
—the latter under English influence. Tea canisters probably came to
Denmark from England. There they were usually kept in a wooden
cabinet along with a sugar bowl. Single cabinets of this type but of

15

Danish origin and dating from the latter part of the century have been preserved (cf. No. 200) but the silver box dating from 1701 (No. 201) is possibly a sugar box from such a cabinet.

Sugar was taken with both tea and coffee, at any rate in the 18th Century. And so there is constant reference to sugar boxes, sugar-bowls and sugar-dishes. But it is usually difficult to decide which of the bowls that have been preserved were used for sugar, or whether for example there was any difference between these and the sweet-dishes which were frequently referred to and which were in general use by the 17th Century. Either sugar-candy or lump-sugar was used; and so sugar-tongs were popular. These are mentioned by the 1720's. The earliest ones were in the form of scissors, but later appeared the sugar-tongs proper (Nos. 494—6) with two sprung arms, usually with spoon-shaped ends. This form became the most popular one by the end of the century.

Sugar was used not only with tea and coffee but also at the dinner-table. It was used in Denmark to sweeten food from the 16th Century; in the 17th Century it is also said to have been used with hot wine —evidently what we would now call toddy; in the 18th Century the inventories mention "wine spoons": these were probably the small spoons with long handles that we now call "toddy spoons" (Nos. 438 and 441). Sugar used at the dinner-table was probably put in vessels like salt-cellars; an order to the Court sugar-refiner in 1680 lays down, inter alia, that he shall supply the salt-cellars ("die Salzfässer") at the King's table with sweets, sugar and condiments. Silver dredgers were evidently used for granulated sugar from the middle of the 17th Century. The oldest surviving one dates from 1677 (No. 205). The earlier sugar-dredgers must all have conformed to the same contemporary English pattern: a cylindrical container with detachable open-work lid. At the beginning of the 18th Century a baluster-shaped or pear-shaped dredger became common, —also after an English design; in the Rococo period the sugar-dredgers acquired three legs like the coffee- and tea-pots; and naturally with the arrival of the neo-classical style they often assumed a vase shape. Towards the end of the 18th Century sugar-dredgers ceased to be used, and sugar-bowls with sugar-sifters were employed instead. Sugar-sifters appeared at the middle of the century.

Salt, like sugar, played its part as a condiment at the dinner-table. Salt food was a main dish in Denmark from pre-historic times, and even during the Renaissance large quantities of salt were used in the preparation and service of food. Silver salt-cellars are mentioned both in the 16th and 17th Centuries; sometimes they were very large, and as a rule, judging by weight specifications at least, they were considerably larger than those of the 18th Century. But it is impossible, among bowls made in the 17th Century to point to one type as being definitely a salt-cellar. The oldest surviving salt-cellar dates from the beginning of the 18th Century (No. 247).

After the discovery of the sea-route to India the consumption of spices increased enormously. It is evident e. g. from the order to the Court sugar-refiner already cited that in the 1680's salt-cellars were also used for spices; and indeed, special spice-bowls are not mentioned in the 17th Century. To this day at the Danish court both salt and pepper are served in salt-cellars according to the old tradition; in the 18th Century there appeared salt-cellars with two compartments, each with lid, for salt and pepper (No. 250). But early in the century began the production of spice-casters, miniature editions of the sugar-dredgers. It was by no means rare for people to have a set of dredgers (or pots) of this kind in silver; in 1719 is listed, among the effects of a Copenhagen citizen, a centre-piece consisting of a salver with sugar-dredger, oil-, vinegar- and mustard-jugs, all in silver. A set which has survived from the beginning of the century (No. 229) consists of a pepper-pot, oil-, vinegar- and mustard-jugs and from the latter part of the century we have a corresponding set with sugar-dredger and salver to match (No. 221). A Swedish cookery-book of 1751 describes how such a salver could be arranged with dredgers and jugs as a central feature of the table service. Salvers were simpler substitutes for cruets (plats-de-menage) which are mentioned in a contemporary account as being central features of the table decoration. This Scandinavian usage of the French word "plat-de-menage" is unknown in France. But the article itself has French prototypes. The beginning of the 18th Century saw the introduction in France of a splendid silver centre-piece with decorative figures, candle-branches, dessert bowls, and dredgers for spices etc. Among the silver plate in the possession of the Danish court in the 18th Century art listed two plats-de-menage of different sizes; the bigger one was designed in the form of a mountain supported on pillars, with a fountain (waterfall) and figures of hunters, stags etc. and likewise equipped with candle-branches, bowls, and all kinds of canisters and dredgers. No such monumental piece has survived, but there were also more simple cruets. A description of one is to be found in the Swedish cookery book of 1751 already mentioned, and similar ones are mentioned, e. g. in the inventory of the estate of a Nykøbing official in 1757: a plat-de-menage consisting of salver, centre-piece, four candle-branches, eight dessert-bowls, two sugar-dredgers, a pepper-caster, and oil- and vinegar-jugs. A cruet dating from 1780 (No. 222, which incidentally is engraved with the name "Plat-de-menage") has no candle-fittings but is crowned with a large sweetmeat-bowl (cf. also centre-piece No. 304); at the close of the century the cruet became the handy and unpretentious frame purely for condiment vessels that we know to-day.

The large plats-de-menage are in a sense perhaps a more precious (and more durable) off-shoot of the show-dishes which were common in the 16th and part of the 17th Centuries, and of the fantastic Baroque table decoration with fountains on the tables and huge elaborate structures with towers and figures of glass, paper and sugar, sometimes embellished with flowers and foliage, the arrangement of which was the job of the King's sugar-refiner.

The sumptuous repasts of the 18th Century followed, broadly speaking, a tradition that derived from the 16th. It was then that cookery was first really practised as an art, with the introduction of many new dishes into the country; at the same time it became the general practice not to put all the food on the table at once but to introduce several courses—usually two or three. Every day at the court of Christian V (1670—99) were consumed twenty-four dishes divided into two courses apart from dessert. Thus many plates of different sizes were needed. Among the new items which appeared in the 16th Century menu were various kinds of soup, which were originally used as gravies accompanying other dishes but soon came to exist in their own right. In inventories of this period may be seen frequent references to silver "salsirkener" (salsaria), indicating gravy- or soup-bowls. Dessert consisted of a sweet (all kinds of sweetmeats, jam or preserved fruits), cakes and fruit. For these also were employed many different kinds of silverware; sweet-bowls, as already mentioned, were listed very often.

Various bowls have survived from the 17th Century, and it is no longer possible to distinguish among them according to function, for they were probably used for several purposes: not a few, indeed, both for eating and drinking. The most common Renaissance type (imitated right up to ca. 1700) is a bowl, usually with low foot and with one handle in the form of a flat lug and the other cast in the

18

form of a pine-cone, cherub's head etc. This is the previously-mentioned "kovsken" which was widespread throughout Scandinavia; the form itself derives from Russia. Other bowls produced in the 16th and 17th Centuries have two flat lugs or two cast, twisted handles. All are found in varying sizes. A bowl made in 1594 (No. 312) has a lid with three balls, probably so that the lid could be used independently as a bowl. A similar lid was found as a rule on a type of bowl which appeared in the last quarter of the 17th Century. It is a large bowl standing on four balls or ball-and-claws (as on the tankards) and with cast, twisted handles, often terminating in grotesque animal heads (Nos. 319—325). This type of bowl is typically Scandinavian; in Sweden, where it is widespread, it is regarded as of Danish origin.

In the 18th Century appeared a new bowl, low, round, without foot but often with a salver to match, which might indicate that the bowl was used for hot fluids (compare the contemporary coffee- and tea-pots). It has often detachable ring- or bow-shaped handles both on the bowl and lid; sometimes there is a wooden grip on the handles, likewise for insulation. These bowls are often called "travelling tureens' (rejseterriner) because similiar bowls are known to have belonged to a cabinet designed for one person's use, possibly when travelling (those examples found in Denmark were usually made in Augsburg). Whether they were more often used instead to hold stews cannot now be established. At the same time as these bowls there appeared the tureen proper, which became the most distinguished item of silver plate in the 18th Century. The tureen comes from France; the word itself does not appear in Denmark before the middle of the Century; instead the expression "soup bowl" is used. Goldsmiths worked on the design and ornament of these masterpieces of the table with no less care and devotion than that lavished on the corresponding articles by the European porcelain and faience factories that were then growing in importance. Tureens often took the place of honour in the centre of the table, surrounded by the other dishes and bowls. Sometimes they were mainly decorative in function; the detachable interiors which, after a French prototype, are to be seen in many of the most splendid tureens were probably used for carrying in the soup from the kitchen, the tureen itself being placed in the middle of the table before the beginning of the meal as the principal decoration. Plans showing the arrangement of the royal tables about 1770 show that tureens were used in this way at the less important meals and for everyday use at the king's own table. But on the big festive occasions the sugar-refiner was still given the privilege of lavishing his skill on the centre of the table. A Danish cookery-book of 1785 refers to the use also of a "mirror-plateau" in the middle of the larger supper-tables; they must certainly have been in use even earlier, and on them were placed the figures which the European porcelain factories were producing in such large numbers for table decoration and other purposes; and they added an extra brilliance to the festive lustre cast by the candelabra over a table laden with silver.

Around the tureen, or whatever now formed the centre of the table, were arranged dishes, plates and salad-bowls in strictly symmetrical order, while lining the edge of the table were long rows of plates. Only a few plates and no dishes have survived from the table services of the 16th and 17th Centuries. Dishes were then, indeed, comparatively numerous. For the wedding of his eldest son, Prince Christian the heir apparent in 1634 Christian IV ordered 300 silver plates and the same number of dishes. A few plates have come down to us from the end of the 16th Century (Nos. 373—74); the richly chased plates made about 1700 (Nos. 375—77) are very thin and were probably only used as salvers—for example for use with drinking glasses, which in the 17th and 18th Centuries were filled at a special sideboard and carried to the table (in other words, glasses were not, as in our day, part of the table service). A single plate dating from ca. 1700 with an obliquely gadrooned border (No. 378) was probably typical, but by about 1740 a type of plate was developed of which many examples have been preserved and which to a certain extent has held its own during successive ages. This has a curved or wavy outline and the rim has a simple grooved moulding (No. 379). The prototype is French; among the Royal Household Silver may still be found French examples dating from the end of the 1730's and the first Danish imitations of them from the beginning of the 1740's. The dishes had a corresponding form, whether round or oval, large or small. It was quite common in the 18th Century for dishes to have a lid to keep the food warm, but only a few such lids have survived. Small three-, four- or six-sided dishes (see Nos. 393—394) in the latter part of the 18th Century are described as "salad-bowls"; these were not only used for salads but also seem to have been employed e. g. in the service of cakes and jam.

In the 18th Century a knife, fork and spoon were placed at the side of each plate. The knife was certainly the oldest eating utensil, but originally was only rarely made with a silver handle —as opposed to the 18th Century, when this was common.

Silver spoons are known to derive from the Middle Ages. At an early date the spoon became the most widespread of all silver articles: even in the 16th Century there were one or more silver spoons in the home of every peasant or citizen of comfortable means. But generally the guests in those days had to bring their own knife and spoon with them; only the houses of the great could provide such things in sufficient quantity. This was the case up to the beginning of the 18th Century, at any rate in the small provincial towns. Sets of spoons of uniform design were in use by the 16th Century; in the effects of a citizen of Elsinore in 1571 are listed eight table-spoons of uniform type; but the fact that this was mentioned implies that it was not the general rule. Silverware buried during the Swedish wars in the 17th Century and since unearthed contains as a rule a motley assortment of spoons (cf. illustration on page 11).

From the Renaissance so much material has survived that one can obtain a fairly clear picture of the various types of spoons and their development. The older Renaissance spoons had as a rule a very short handle and a round or pear- (fig-) shaped bowl; the handle usually terminated in a finial which in the 16th Century was often polygonal or round as in the Middle Ages. Sometimes the finial was a cast figure, or the whole handle could be cast in the form of a Virgin etc. From the end of the 16th Century onwards may be found a type of spoon of which the finial is cast in the form of a cherub head; these "Cherub spoons" continued to be made until after 1700. Rather like these are spoons with a scrolled finial in a form reminiscent of cherubs. At the beginning of the 17th Century there appear, almost as often as "cherub spoons", the "grape spoons" ("drueskeerne") with a finial in the form of a pine-cone or a bunch of grapes. All these types of spoon have a round or polygonal handle. One may also meet with spoons made in the early 17th Century with a handle of which the outer half is flat (e. g. No. 406); as time went on the whole handle became flat; this became common by the middle of the 17th Century; at the same time the handle became broader with a straight or rounded end; the stem often terminated in a flower cast in relief, of which the stalk and leaf could be indicated by an engraving on the stem. Towards the end of the century a trifid-ended flat stem became common: the oldest example dates probably from the late 1660's (No. 429). The bowl of the spoon now became more oval, a form that was retained until late in the following century. At the same time the stem often continued down the back of the bowl in the form of a pointed spine—the so-called "rat-tail" which certainly derived from England and is most probably a reminiscence of the 17th Century spoons with bowls of agate or other precious stones; these bowls were attached to the stem by a similar prolongation of the stem below the bowl. The "rat-tail" survived until the 18th Century but completely disappeared with the arrival of Rococo. On spoons dating from the last years of its vogue the "rat-tail" may be seen merely indicated as an engraving on the bowl. The trifid end was replaced about 1700 by a wavy end, the middle lobe being preserved as a pointed tongue on the end of the handle.

In the Rococo period spoons had a rounded end; the stem itself took the form of a fiddle or an oar, usually with a threaded edge and terminating in a cast leaf ornament or a Rococo shell. The earliest known examples of this type in Denmark were made for the Royal Household Silver in 1741 after French patterns. In many cases the handle is quite plain or decorated with a small engraved or stamped Rococo ornament, which may also be seen on the under-side of the bowl. At the end of the century the latter usually took the shape of a pointed oval and the handle had a corresponding lancet shape. In the 1790's the handle was often covered with engraved ornament: the typical so-called "Empire" spoon appeared after contemporary English prototypes (of the "Old English" pattern); it continued in general use in the first quarter of the 19th Century. But the simplest Rococo type of spoon never went out of use. Along with it appeared (about 1830) a plain spoon decorated only with a cast shell on the end of the handle; this too was certainly inspired by 18th Century models.

The only types of forks which are known to have been used in Denmark before 1600 were carving forks. In 1621 Christian IV mentions the purchase of one fork, and when silver forks are mentioned in 17th Century inventories it is always in quite small quantities. Woven in a table-cloth from Christian IV's silk factory in 1621 may be seen an illustration of a table laid for a meal, with a two-pronged fork by each person's plate. But even if this picture gives a true picture of conditions in Denmark at the time the question of using silver forks at any rate did not arise; in 1622 there were 63 silver spoons in Christian IV's Household Silver but no silver forks. Most probably the earlier forks had as a general rule two iron prongs and a handle of agate or other material. From the 1660's have survived some gold forks with four prongs (Nos. 421 and 430); the handle has precisely the same form as the contemporary spoons, and this continues to be the case when one begins to find forks more and more widespread. Normally these forks have three prongs, and four prongs do not become general until the end of the 18th Century.

From the 17th Century onwards spoons and forks were made in pairs for single persons. It is doubtful if a single instance could be found of a complete set of silver knives, forks and spoons designed as a unit before the Royal Household Silver authorities at the beginning of the 1740's obtained the service previously mentioned as having been based on French designs.

There were special eating utensils in addition to the standard ones: carving knives and forks with silver handles were referred to as early as the 16th Century; in 1623 the Mayor of Elsinore was in possession of a dessert fork; tea-spoons came along with tea- and coffee-pots; the wine- and toddy-spoons already mentioned were referred to in a will made at Elsinore in 1737, but most probably were already in existence before this date. Along with the soup bowls came soup-ladles; a large spoon known to exist by 1740 is sometimes called a porridge-spoon but also a serving spoon—it was part of the carver's equipment; and when at about the middle of the 18th Century it became customary to produce complete sets of eating utensils, there appeared also dessert sets consisting of small knives, forks and spoons, the knives and forks often having porcelain handles. All these articles were made in the same styles as the ordinary eating utensils. Rather different were the cream-ladles and sugar-sifters already discussed, while the punch-ladles dating from the middle of the 18th Century usually resembled large cream-ladles (sometimes with a strainer); fish-slices and cake-spoons from the same period were shaped like flat spades.

These remarks, which can only be regarded as a sketchy outline of the history of domestic silver in Denmark, will have given some impression, on the one hand of the very limited range of types of silver in the 16th and 17th Centuries and on the other of the increasing specialisation according to function that took place after 1700. So far as concerns the types of silver at our disposal as well as the manner of using them we are still living in the traditions of the 18th Century. A better impression of the whole subject will be gained by studying the following illustrations: but the subject is understood best of all by those who themselves know the joy of handling a fine old silver piece and using it at their own table.

In the foregoing pages an attempt has been made to describe the various types of silverware made for domestic use and their development, and at the same time to say something about the way in which they were used. A few remarks may be added in conclusion about the decoration applied to silverware at various periods: they are obviously intended as broad generalisations rather than a penetrating stylistic analysis.

The goldsmiths of the Danish Renaissance (ca. 1550—1650) preferred engraving to chasing as a form of decoration. Gadrooning appears for example on goblets (e. g. No. 34), but generally speaking engraved ornaments were used on all types of silverware. In isolated cases a definite ornament engraving was evidently used as a pattern, but more often the goldsmiths drew upon the rich common stock of Renaissance designs, especially under Dutch and German influence: rolled cartouches, studded ornaments, bunches of fruit and stylised plant tendrils. Frequently there appears a chequered or lozengy border, e. g. in the moulded base of the tankard. Ornaments cast in relief were used very often, especially in the central panel in the lid of the tankard and as a thumb-piece; cast cherub-heads were used as a finial on spoons or adorned the rings surrounding tankards and beakers.

The so-called "auricular style" (see note to No. 16), which especially dominated Danish wood-carving in the mid-decades of the 17th Century, had apparently only a limited influence on the goldsmith's art: only odd pieces engraved or chased in this style are known to exist. But after the middle of the century the Baroque style came storming in with its bold acanthus leaves and large naturalistic flowers. These were engraved especially on the lids of tankards and bowls, while the remainder of the piece concerned was often left with plain surfaces, possibly relieved by an engraved coat-of-arms or a flower-wreath surrounding a monogram. The Baroque style brought with it a sense of contrasted effects between parts that were richly decorated and others where the material revealed its own beauty and set off the form. Similiar effects may be seen for instance on spoons. Chased decoration, in contrast to engraving, became more common

24

as time went on. Leaves and flowers, especially in the last twenty or thirty years of the century, were often boldly chased; sometimes chased ornaments covered the whole piece, in the German style, but as a rule only certain parts were decorated, on tankards especially the lids and the area above each foot. A special, more simple decoration (especially employed on beakers) appeared about the middle of the 17th Century; the sides of the silver piece were matted with a punch, while the edges and often a round or oval panel left over in the middle of the side was smoothly polished. In the open panel was engraved a name or a coat-of-arms (see e. g. Nos. 63 or 316). Beakers with this decoration were still produced throughout the 18th Century.

About the year 1700 chased acanthus leaves and flowers became lighter (e. g. No. 23). The florid Baroque style, which had marked Dutch characteristics, was supplanted by lighter and more elegant French designs, and at the same time appeared the French-inspired strapwork, which early in the following century practically reigned supreme in chased decoration. This is a type of ornament deriving from ornament engravings, especially of Jean Bérain, and consists mainly of a straight or curved band with right-angle joins, delicate acanthus leaves sheathing the edges of the band and pendent campanula-flowers (e. g. Nos. 28 and 177). Strapwork is met with in isolated instances on silverware by the 1690's, but it became especially common from about 1715 and was used right up to about the middle of the century; it is in a sense typical of one aspect of late Danish Baroque, which is often misleadingly called Regency, even though to a very limited extent one can speak of similarities between the two styles. Late Danish Baroque, however, uses more parallel lines.

There was an English as well as a French influence during this period. This is revealed in a detail of decoration such as gadrooning, which was in general use especially from about 1690 to 1720 both as a surface ornament (e. g. No. 230) or in the form of narrow borders (e. g. Nos. 207 and 208). English influence also appears in the fondness for plain silverware which may often be seen in the period about 1700 and the decades following; here the richest decoration consisted of engraved initials or coat-of-arms. One can find points of comparison with features of the early Danish Baroque mentioned above, but it is certainly not due to accident that the plain silverware of the late Baroque often consists of objects of English design, as for example some of the early tea canisters.

Not much study has been given to the connection between English and Danish art at that time. Danish craftsmanship (not only silverware but also e. g. furniture) of the late 17th and the beginning of the 18th Century shows a great deal of English influence. On the other hand a certain Danish influence appears in English silverware of the late 17th Century, when tankards of the Danish-Norwegian pattern were made in Newcastle and York.

While silver with these plain surfaces continued to be produced throughout the first half of the century, there appeared in the 1720's a new stylistic feature in the shape of fluting, which made its mark throughout Northern and Central Europe but was especially cultivated in Denmark. In fluted silverware the surface, which is usually undecorated, is broken into vertical, parallel grooves, with a concave and convex groove side by side; usually the grooves are arranged in groups of two (rarely three) such double-grooves, so that the first double-groove is concave-convex, the next convex-concave, and the surface between them often appears as a broad band running down the side of the object (e. g. Nos. 132—33 and 157). Fluting of this straight type disappeared from Copenhagen silverware about the middle of the century, but remained nevertheless in many provincial areas. In some places it then became customary to decorate the plain surfaces between the grooves especially with chased Rococo shells, which often were quite clumsy, so that it becomes possible to speak of a special Provincial Rococo; this was seen especially in Aalborg (e. g. Nos. 107 and 135) but also in other North Jutland towns (e. g. Randers—cf. No. 277). A cast bird, which was generally used as a finial in the Rococo period, also acquired a special development in Aalborg, where it nearly always had outspread wings (e. g. No. 135).

In about 1740 the Rococo style began to appear in Denmark. Its arrival was heralded by the design of the interiors of the new Christiansborg Castle and by the manufacture at about the same time of a silver service for the Court, in part at least revealing French influence. A tureen from this service (No. 333) shows a transitional style in fluted silver. The flutings still run vertically, but they appear in groups of three, of which two look like gently swelling protuberances running down the side of the vessel while the third is pressed in like a sharp fold between them. The softer lines now matched the profusely curved outlines.

From about 1750, with the introduction of twisted fluting, the flowing lines of the Rococo style and its lack of symmetry became the dominant influence on Copenhagen silver (and gradually on that made in the provinces also).

Here the flutings were traced in curved lines over the softly rounded surface, and horizontal lines and moulding were as far as possible eliminated. The handles, legs etc. were embellished with irregular cast and chased Rococo shells. Apart from the flutings, surfaces were left as a rule undecorated, but sometimes one comes across Rococo silver with twisted fluting and richly decorated with chased Rococo shells and flowers (e. g. No. 164). Twisted fluting flourished during the period ca. 1750—75, but in the following decade also it was possible to produce various pieces in this style.

But the Rococo style was not confined to twisted fluting (which originally showed German influence). A smaller group of objects were inspired by French models, with plain curved surfaces and cast Rococo shells and matted vines. On some of these and corresponding pieces made in the 1760's may be seen a style of ornament, often matted, which is indeed linked with early French Rococo but is especially reminiscent of the Bérain ornament in late Baroque. One finds especially an ornament like a C on its side, a small campanula and a crucifer flower and around the foot of the piece a circle of small bows or tongues that remind one of the gadrooning of the late Baroque period (and of the neo-classical period that followed).

This decoration, which is symmetrical and is often found along with grooved rims with cross-bands, the classical "fasces", was possibly an outcome of the reaction against the disintegrating tendencies of Rococo, which under the leadership of the French architect N. Jardin made its impression in other branches of Danish-craftsmanship about 1760, earlier than in most other countries. The idea was to look back rather to the classical tendencies in late Baroque than to the style of antiquity. One may perhaps apply to this kind of ornament the tentative name of "early neo-classical" (cf. for instance Nos. 139 and 165). Silverware in the proper neo-classical style (the so-called Louis Seize style) did not begin to be produced in Copenhagen until the 1770's. These articles often assumed a vase- or pillar-shape, but frequently retain something of the soft, curved lines of the Rococo period; they were decorated with "fasces" rims and bead edgings or chased acanthus leaves, festoons and medallions, radial gadrooning around the lower part of the vase and meander motifs (e. g. Nos. 166—167).

About 1790 this neo-classicism changed its character, as a result especially of influence deriving from England, which exported a large number of plated goods to Denmark at this time. While pieces affected by this influence were often barrel-shaped or cylindrical the ornamentation usually took the form of delicate engraving instead of chasing (e. g. No. 121)—unless the design was left plain and undecorated (e. g. Nos. 144—145); often openwork was employed with usually a blue glass liner as background. English influence continued to take effect in the first quarter of the 19th Century, the so-called "Empire" period, which has nothing to do with the ruling fashions of the French imperialist age. Usually on Copenhagen silverware from ca. 1805 to 1820 may be seen a chased border of leaves (vines, acanthus, etc.) with shield cartouches. Many silver articles dating from this period rest on curved legs with lion paws on a base with four concave, curved sides and ball feet (e. g. No. 173). Openwork was still cultivated but also thread- and filigree-work were employed (e. g. Nos. 261 and 399). After 1820 designs became more academically classical, ornament became more severe and confined itself to chased fluting, palmette borders and acanthus leaves (e. g. No. 297). Even in the earliest years of the neo-classical movement it happened that contemporary artists (e. g. Johannes Wiedewelt) made drawings for the use of the goldsmiths; the silverware of the late Danish Empire period was influenced by the designs of one man. The architect G. F. Hetsch was a pupil of Percier, one of the leading artists of the French Empire style; from the middle of the 1820's until about 1840 he influenced Danish craftsmanship to such an extent that the French academic classical style remained in Denmark longer than anywhere else (cf. No. 149). Not until after 1840 did the new Rococo, which had long before become dominant abroad, take root in Denmark. With it begins, also so far as concerns silverware, the period of mixed styles with the results of which this book is not concerned.

Portion of a white damask table-cloth, woven at Christian IV' silk factory in Copenhagen 1621 (now at Rosenborg Castle). The middle of the cloth shows a table laid for a meal, as seen from above; in the centre are arranged a number of large dishes with wild fowl, fish and tarts, flanked by smaller dishes with fish, crab and fruit; in between are small dishes with fruit, jam etc. (Dishes of widely different types were served together with each course). By each plate is a piece of bread, a knife and a two-pronged fork. Flowers are strewn on the table. — The table-cloth is photographed off the straight so that the pattern can stand out from the white damask.

In Denmark, as elsewhere, the art of the goldsmith is an old one. Antiquarian discoveries show us what the goldsmiths were capable of producing, but they do not reveal whether the pieces concerned were imported or of domestic manufacture.

At an early period goldsmiths were employed by the Church to produce ecclesiastical plate and other Church furnishings; but wordly interests also claimed their services. In Bishop Absalon's will (1201) are mentioned silver bowls, beakers, and plates. The first goldsmiths whose names we know for certain lived in the 12th century. In 1429 King Erik of Pomerania (1412—39) gave the goldsmiths of Copenhagen their first charter, which contained a series of provisions for the complete regulation of the goldsmiths' gild with regard to the respective status of masters, journeymen, and apprentices, and regulations intended to assure the public of proper workmanship, especially in the matter of "gehalt" (purity), i. e. how much base metal (mainly copper) might be mixed with gold and silver. How high the standard of purity must be is not stated directly, since the charter does not mention definite figures but only speaks of standard silver and standard gold.

In 1491 King Hans issued an ordinance in which the legal standard of purity of silver was fixed, so that each "mark" ($=$ 16 "lod") should contain $14\frac{1}{4}$ lod of pure silver and $1\frac{3}{4}$ lod of alloy. At the same time goldsmiths were ordered to put their maker's mark and the hall-mark of the town on all new silver-work they produced. This order was repeated in the Copenhagen goldsmiths' charter of 1496.

The gilds arose when the division of labour had progressed so far that a man could earn a living by devoting himself to a definite trade. The authorities were concerned to ensure the interests of both craftsmen and consumers and to this end they issued certain ordinances for the various gilds. In the beginning it was scarcely difficult to secure acceptance as a gild member, but as competition increased more stringent conditions were introduced concerning the training of apprentices and journeymen's examination and later, compulsory masters' examinations. The period of training lasted from five to seven years. When the apprentice became a journeyman he must travel for some years before he could become a master. These years were important, since they gave the journeyman the chance of studying conditions of work in other countries and of bringing home new ideas. But by degrees the gilds used their monopoly powers to force up prices and to limit the admittance of new members. In the 18th Century there was a gradual change in public opinion about the gilds; more and more people obtained Royal permission to carry on business outside them, and by the close of the century there was a powerful movement in favour of a complete abolition of the gild ordinances. The Government dared not go so far as this, however. Although the "free master" system was extended by a journeyman of four years standing being given the right to set himself up as a master outside the gild —but without being able to keep a journeyman— no great relief was provided. Not until the Trade Act of 1857 was the gild system abolished to clear the path for freedom of commerce.

As a rule there was only one goldsmith in the smaller provincial towns, and he was a member of the blacksmiths' gilds. Only in Aalborg, Aarhus and Odense were there separate goldsmiths' gilds.

In the 16th and 17th Centuries were issued many Royal ordinances to the goldsmiths' gilds tightening up the relevant provisions as to standards of purity and thus indicating that more than a little swindling actually took place. When a customer wanted a piece of work done he must usually himself supply the necessary raw material (coins or discarded silver articles) to the goldsmith. The latter was, however, obliged to ensure that his finished article was up to the legal standard even though the raw material supplied had been below it. Law cases relating to silver not complying with the standards figure as frequent entries in the Court records of the country.

Even though Copenhagen, the biggest town in Denmark, had the greatest number of goldsmiths, there were many in the bigger provincial towns, and they were not outshone in skill by those of the capital. Didrik Fuiren, who lived in Odense in the second half of the 16th Century, was certainly one of the most able goldsmiths of his day. His most famous work is Christian IV's crown, which is to be seen at Rosenborg Castle. He is considered to have been very prosperous, which is more than can be said of most of his colleagues. In prestige the goldsmiths' was the most distinguished of the craftsmen's gilds and ranked next after the merchants'. From contemporary records it appears that gold and silver, both in their raw and manufactured states, were generally used as a means of payment, and goldsmiths, in addition to practising their craft, used to handle exchange business.

The 17th Century was a good time for goldsmiths. While apart from Church altar-cups and a number of spoons only a few examples of work have been preserved from earlier periods, a large number of pieces are known to date from the 17th Century, and we also know the names of most of the goldsmiths who produced them. Of the goldsmiths of that period may be named: Steen Pedersen, Alexander Traegaard, Carsten Lauridsen, Johan Stichmann, Jørgen Stilcke, Johan Kohlmann, and Jean Henry de Moor in Copenhagen, Hermand Jensen in Aalborg, Dionis Willadsen in Næstved, Anders Jensen, Simon Mathiesen and Jesper Rust in Odense.

In 1685 was issued a new charter for the Copenhagen goldsmiths' gild; this, by and large, remained in force up to the middle of the 19th Century. It was here provided that all pieces over 75 grams weight should be stamped by a surveyor (the "guardein"), an official named by the king, who in addition to his own mark should put the Copenhagen hall-mark on all pieces which were up to the legal standard. (From 1608 the Copenhagen hall-mark contained the three towers represented in the coat-of-arms of the city and a date, so that it had to be changed every year). The legal standard was now fixed so that each "mark" should contain $13^1/_3$ "lod" of pure silver and $2^2/_3$ "lod" of alloy. At the same time appear the so-called "month marks" which give the month in which the piece concerned was approved. Until the beginning of the 19th Century the signs of the Zodiac were used, and later on naturalistic reproductions of the animals of the Zodiac. As a fourth mark on Copenhagen silver appears the maker's mark. In the provinces it was customary for only the maker's mark to be used; the prescribed hall-mark was only exceptionally employed.

The charter referred to above contains also a provision that goldsmiths should change their mark every year. This was often done in practice by adding a date underneath the maker's mark. But many ignored this ruling either completely or in part.

In the 18th Century the Copenhagen goldsmiths were in advance of those from the provinces. In the Rococo period in particular they could point to a considerable number of outstanding pieces which outshone by their richness and elegance those produced in the provinces. But many of the goldsmiths of the bigger towns produced work that could compare favourably with the best Copenhagen ware.

Of the Copenhagen goldsmiths of the 18th Century may be named: Isak Dubois, Niels Johnsen, Fridrich Fabritius, Jens Pedersen Komløv, Nicolai Junge, Jens Christensen, Ole Flores Wilcken, Asmus

Fridrich Holling, Christopher Jonsen, Sivert Thorsteinsson, Detleff Pape, Thomas Andreas Westrup, Christian Werum and Christian Hosøe. Of the provincial goldsmiths may be named: Mikkel Jensen, Laurids Holm, Jens Kieldsen Sommerfeldt and Hans Busch in Aalborg, Johan Henriksen Plumb and Johannes Zönnichsen Buxlund in Aarhus, Mogens Thommesen Løwenhertz and Knud Brandt in Horsens, Jørgen Friis and Peter Norman in Randers and Rasmus Møller in Odense.

In the 19th Century the effect of industrialisation became more and more marked, and when free trade was introduced the gilds were dissolved. Two of the best-known Copenhagen goldsmiths of the first half of this century were Abraham Nyemann and Jørgen Balthazar Dalhoff.

Our knowledge of the goldsmiths' workshops and their equipment is derived mainly from pictures. Sometimes the workshops were divided into two rooms, one for the rougher work such as smelting, casting, wire-drawing and the rougher forging and the other for the more delicate work such as chasing, engraving, small soldering work and the final polishing. But more often all the work was done in one room.

Since both gold and silver in their pure form are too soft for practical use they have to be alloyed with another metal, mostly copper. This process was carried out in enclosed draught-ovens with a natural draught, or in furnaces in which the supply of air was increased by the use of bellows (in smaller furnaces, a blow-pipe). The fuel used was charcoal. Smelting took place in crucibles of graphite or fireproof clay. The molten metal was poured into ingot moulds corresponding to the shapes into which it was to be forged. Then the real work of the goldsmith began as the metal was hammered into shape. (Casting work was done too, but here the metal after cooling had to be worked over with an engraving tool and polisher).

In the workshop was a bench consisting of a heavy board indented with a large space for each workman. The workman sat fairly low and in order to collect the precious filings a skin of calf-leather was always hung below the bench in front of each workman. A heavy wooden block was put on the table to support the piece being worked upon. Illumination was poor by modern standards; it consisted of a tallow candle behind a glass ball filled with water to focus the light on the limited area of operations. There was also a vice for holding the many various shapes of iron used in the course of work. A hammer was the goldsmith's most important tool, and it was reckoned that an apprentice needed twenty or thirty different shapes of hammer. There were forge hammers with a flat surface at one end and a flat wedge at the other, designed for hammering out the ingot to a sheet. There were also long, narrow hammers used for hollowing out. In this process the silver was placed on the anvil in sheet form and hammered out from the middle towards the edges, and the material thus began to assume the form of a cup. Another type of hammer was used for planishing or beating out the vessel over an iron stake made for the purpose. There were also hammers for smoothing and other special jobs. During the forging process the silver had to be kept at a high temperature so that it remained sufficiently malleable, and iron moulds of different sizes were used as a bed. The workshop's equipment included other necessary implements such as files of many different shapes and sizes for levelling and smoothing, drills, fret-saws, and pliers for clipping and soldering.

Surface decoration consisted of chasing and engraving. Fluting, both straight and twisted, which was a special feature of late Baroque and Rococo was done by first hammering out the object (e. g. coffee-pot) in the rough and then hammering its sides into grooves over a curved piece of iron held in a vice. Chasing could be used as an additional form of decoration if it was desired to adorn the surface with raised figures such as flowers, fruits, animals etc. In order to secure sufficient support for the work the silver was placed on a pitch block, or the inside of the vessel itself was filled with pitch: this ensured a foundation which was not only firm but malleable. The upper surface could then be worked by driving variously shaped punches against it with light blows of a hammer. These punches, which were rather like a form of chisel, were required in various sizes and with variously shaped ends. If it was required to indent the surface of the silver at a point inaccessible to an ordinary punch a snarling-iron could be used, consisting of a steel rod with an angle bend, the shorter arm ending in a knob, while the longer arm was made fast in a vice. By hammering near the fixed end the rod could be made to vibrate and thus the knob could indent the surface of the vessel held against it. The process of engraving consisted of using an engraving scorper to cut figures in the upper surface of the object. The engraving scorper is a well-tempered steel rod with one end sharpened to a cutting point. A lathe was also part of the workshop's equipment.

Wire was made by drawing the ingot through a number of conical holes in a steel draw-plate until the required thickness was required.

Soldering, a difficult process, since one had to be very careful to avoid over-heating, was done with the aid of a blow-pipe or over a slow fire. Since the silver and the soldering metal had about the same melting point great care was needed. As a means of keeping the soldered area clean borax was used.

Gilding in the old days consisted of the so-called "fire-gilding" which was not replaced by galvanised gilding until 100 years ago. An amalgam of gold and quicksilver was made and spread evenly over the surface, which had been well cleaned beforehand, after which the quicksilver was heated and steamed away leaving the gold behind as a thin layer. The quicksilver vapour was highly poisonous and must have ruined the health of many goldsmiths.

The final touch was given to the work by filing and polishing. The silver was treated with wet grinding-dust applied finer and finer untill all scratches and roughnesses had disappeared; if the most brilliant possible finish was desired it could be obtained by treating the polished surface with a smooth piece of steel or with a blood-stone.

Left, a proof of a common Copenhagen mark dating from the 18th Century. Above is the Copenhagen hall-mark with the date 1740 and the mark of the royal surveyor ("guardein") P. N. v. Haven; below is the master's mark of Niels Johnsen's widow and "month mark" (the sign of the Virgin governing the period 21st August—23rd September). — Right, an Aarhus mark from the end of the 17th Century with the Aarhus hall-mark and the mark of the goldsmith Erik Andersen Winther. While Copenhagen silver after 1685 usually has four marks as shown here, provincial work is often stamped with the maker's mark alone.

MARKS, NAMES OF PRIVATE OWNERS, AND BIBLIOGRAPHY

In the lists given below the first figure refers to the number of the text accompanying each picture.

The Copenhagen hall-mark is represented by KM (Københavns Mærke) followed by a date; other marks by a B and a number referring to the number of the corresponding mark in C. A. Bøje: Danske guld- og sølvsmedemærker (1946). The mark of the royal surveyor (»guardein«) is only mentioned when it is of any importance in confirming an otherwise uncertain date.

The names referred to in the numbered lists below are the names of present owners. When these are given without the town of origin, this is to be read as Copenhagen. Some owners have asked to remain anonymous. Information about the location of pieces in public ownership is given in the text accompanying the appropriate picture. The museums and collections thus mentioned are:

The Royal Household Silver (Det Kongelige Sølvkammer). — The Danish National Museum, Copenhagen. — The Danish Museum of Decorative Art (Kunstindustrimuseet), Copenhagen. — The C. L. David Collection, Copenhagen. — The Copenhagen Municipal Museum (Bymuseet), Copenhagen. — Rosenborg i. e. The Chronological Collection of the Danish Kings at Rosenborg Castle, Copenhagen. — Frederiksborg i. e. The Museum of Danish National History at Frederiksborg Castle, Hillerød. — »Den gamle By« (The Old Town Museum), Aarhus. — Historical Museum, Aalborg. — Koldinghus i. e. The Museum at Koldinghus Castle, Kolding. — Odense Museum (Historical Museum in Møntergaarden), Odense. — The Museum of Applied Art (Kunstindustrimuseet), Oslo. — Nordiska Museet, Stockholm. — Victoria and Albert Museum, London.

The literary references do not claim to be exhaustive; abbreviations are as follows:

Nyrop = C. Nyrop: Meddelelser om dansk Guldsmedekunst (1885).

D. og S. = J. Olrik: Drikkehorn og Sølvtøj (1909).

D. S. A. = J. Olrik: Danske Sølvarbejder fra Renaissancen til vore Dage (1915).

O. = J. Olrik: Danske Guldsmedes Mærker (1919).

H. Schmitz = H. Schmitz: Generaldirektør Ole Olsens Samling (no date).

Dansk kunsth. = Dansk Kunsthaandværk gennem 400 Aar. Kunstindustrimuseets Jubilæumsudstilling 1946. Katalog. (400 Years of Danish Craftsmanship. Exhibition in the Danish Museum of Decorative Art 1946).

Mit b. ku. = Mit bedste Kunstværk. Udstilling i Statens Museum for Kunst 1941. Katalog. (My best work of art. Exhibition in The Royal Museum of Fine Art, Copenhagen, 1941).

London No. = No. in the catalogue of the exhibition of Danish Art Treasures. Victoria and Albert Museum, London. 1948.

For pieces belonging to the Frederiksborg Museum the reader is referred to the Museum's Catalogue, 2nd edition (1943).

In addition to the works mentioned above the following books and treatises on Danish silver have been used in the preparation of this volume:

P. R. Hinnerup: Haandbog for Juvelere, Guld- og Sølvarbejdere (1839).

Jørgen Olrik: Borgerlige Hjem i Helsingør for 300 Aar siden (1903).

Jørgen Olrik: Nyerhvervet Sølvtøj i Nationalmuseets 2. Afdeling (in Fra Arkiv og Museum. 1911).

Jørgen Olrik: Dansk guldsmedekunst (in Tidsskrift for Industri. 1911).

H. C. Bering Liisberg: Christian IV og Guldsmedene (1929).

J. Olrik in Fra Nationalmuseets Arbejdsmark 1929 og 1932.

M. Mackeprang in Fra Nationalmuseets Arbejdsmark 1930.

Erik Lassen and Ole Wanscher: A. Michelsen og dansk Sølvsmedekunst (1941).

C. A. Bøje: Gammelt dansk sølvtøj (1947).

Erik Lassen: Sølvtøj (in C. L. Davids Samling. Nogle Studier. 1948).

1. B. 123. London No. 196.
2. No marks. Messrs. Berg Bros.
3. B. 3055.
4. B. 3060.
5. No marks.
6. Odense hall-mark and O. 625. Count Moltke, Bregentved. — D. S. A. No. 3. Dansk kunsth. No. 24.
7. Odense hall-mark and master's mark DH or PH.
8. KM 1639 and B. 142. H. Tobiesen, Esq.
9. Aarhus hall-mark (B. 1338) and B. 1354. London No. 202. (In this catalogue the tankard is dated »about 1660«; the right date would probably be somewhere in the 1640's. See »Fra Arkiv og Museum« 1911 pp. 467—469).
10. B. 2929. (This is in effect the master's mark of Hans Olufsen — mentioned B. page 426).
11. B. 1902.
12. B. 167.
13. B. 2262. J. Giersing, Esq.
14. Odense hall-mark and B. 2253. Dansk kunsth. No. 43.
15. B. 169. V. Steensen-Leth, Esq., Steensgaard.
16. B. 1244 and 1258. C. A. Bøje, Esq. Mit b. ku. No. 358. London No. 213.
17. Næstved hall-mark and B. 2173. Count Wedell, Wedellsborg.
18. KM 1671. B. 174.
19. B. 160.
20. B. 1663.
21. Aalborg hall-mark (B. 1245) and B. 1270. Mus. No. 757/1946.
22. B. 2985. Hj. Bruhn, Esq.
23. B. 1798. London No. 210.
24. B. 1270.
25. KM 1722 and B. 331.
26. B. 1798. Count Wedell, Wedellsborg.
27. B. 1369. Count Wedell, Wedellsborg.
28. B. 1281. H. Tobiesen, Esq.
29. B. 1378.
30. B. 1911.
31. Vejle hall-mark for 1756 and B. 2932. Tage Hansen, Esq.
32. B. 1287.
33. KM 1753 and B. 404. Hj. Bruhn, Esq.
34. Køge hall-mark (B. 1950) and B. 1957.
35. B. 1708.
36. B. 3060.
37. B. 1707. London No. 203.
38. KM 1610 and B. 137.
39. KM 1610 and B. 137.
40. B. 3065. Messrs. Berg Bros.
41. B. 2254. Hj. Bruhn, Esq. D. S. A. No. 35.
42. B. 2179. H. Drucker, Esq.
43. B. 131. D. og S. p. 67 No. 14.
44. No marks. D. og S. p. 131.
45. No marks. D. og S. p. 132.
46. B. p. 177.
47. B. 167. Mus. cat. 1943 No. 3304, 3.
48. No marks.
49. B. 2255. (The identification of this mark by Bøje is probably wrong). D. og S. pp. 116—17.
50. B. 152. Mus. No. D. 2868.
51. The maker's mark is not illustrated by Bøje. D. og S. p. 131.
52. B. 1258. Messrs. Berg Bros.
53. No marks. D. og S. pp. 113—14.
54. B. 1353. D. og S. p. 121.
55. No marks. D. og S. p. 67 No. 17.
56. B. 3065. Nyrop fig. 43. D. S. A. No. 36. Dansk kunsth. No. 29.
57. No marks. D. og S. p. 72 No. 29.
58. KM 1654 and B. 172.
59. KM 1654 and B. 183.
60. B. 189.
61. B. 173.
62. B. 2262. D. og S. p. 133.
63. Master's mark SV, not illustrated by Bøje. Mus. cat. 1943, No. 3304, 9.
64. Kalundborg hall-mark, KM 1689 and B. 1868. Mus. cat. 1943, No. 3304, 22.
65. B. 1272. C. A. Bøje, Esq.
66. B. 1260. D. og S. p. 78 No. 46.
67. B. 2979.
68. KM 1698 and B. 220. H. Tobiesen, Esq.
69. Master's mark (PHI?) not illustrated by Bøje. Baron A. G. T. Reedtz-Thott, Gavnø. D. S. A. No. 126.
70. KM 1688 and B. 240. H. Drucker, Esq.
71. KM 1696 and B. 210. D. S. A. No. 135.
72. KM 1705 and B. p. 53 (No. 262 with date 1700). H. Tobiesen, Esq.
73. B. p. 193 (the mark is not illustrated).
74. KM 1692 and B. 253.
75. B. page 413 (most like B. 2832). Mrs. Carl Oppen.
76. No marks (cf. B. page 60). Dansk kunsth. No. 54. London No. 218.
77. B. 1798. London No. 211.
78. B. 312. London No. 218.
79. KM 1733 and B. 348. Hj. Bruhn, Esq.
80. KM 1702 and B. page 74 (the mark is not illustrated). H. Drucker, Esq.
81. KM 1735 and B. 337. Count Wedell, Wedellsborg.
82. KM 1756 and B. 464. H. Drucker, Esq.
83. B. 1379.
84. KM 1769 and B. 573. H. Drucker, Esq.
85. KM 1709 and B. page 58 (another mark than B. 297). D. og S. page 79 No. 51.
86. B. 2268. Baron A. G. T. Reedtz-Thott, Gavnø, D. S. A. No. 159.
87. No marks. Mus. cat. 1943 No. 3304, 12.
88. No marks. London No. 218.
89. KM 1716 and B. 321.
90. KM 1686 and B. 174.
91. KM 1708 and B. 262.
92. B. 610.
93. B. 1805.
94. B. 2415.
95. B. page 198 (the mark is not illustrated).
96. B. 1404.
97. No marks.
98. B. 1361. H. Schmitz No. 402.
99. KM 1732 and B. 340.
100. KM 1717 and master's mark NCI 1715 (cf. B. page 62; the mark is not illustrated).
101. KM 1718 and 327. Hans Bagger, Esq. Dansk kunsth. No. 55.

102. KM 1719 and B. 328.
103. KM 1727 and B. 340. Mrs. Ingegerd Hoff.
104. B. 2410. Mrs. Else Oluf Thomsen.
105. B. 1282. C. A. Bøje, Esq.
106. B. 1282. Mrs. Olsen, Hasseris.
107. B. 1282. H. Drucker, Esq.
108. Master's mark SB (cf. B. page 335; the mark is not illustrated). P. Wedel-Heinen, Esq., Elvedgaard.
109. KM 1749 and B. 372. H. Drucker, Esq.
110. KM 175.. (the last figure illegible) and B. 341. H. Drucker, Esq.
111. KM 1756 and B. 449. H. Tobiesen, Esq.
112. KM 1766 and master's mark AHS (cf. B. page 88; the mark is not illustrated). H. Drucker, Esq.
113. KM 1763 and B. 491.
114. B. 1805. Messrs. Berg Bros.
115. KM 1781 and B. 623. Count W. Knuth, Egeløkke.
116. KM 1779 and B. 531. H. Drucker, Esq.
117. KM 1761 and B. 495.
118. B. 2419.
119. KM 1801 and B. 651. Countess Fanny Rantzau, Krengerup.
120. KM (the date and the master's mark are illegible). H. Drucker, Esq.
121. KM 1798 and B. 742. J. M. Valeur, Esq.
122. KM 1790 and one of the marks B. 654—57. Formerly in the Ole Olsen Collection. H. Schmitz, No. 506.
123. KM 1812.
124. KM 1821 and B. 879. H. Tobiesen, Esq.
125. KM 1830 and B. 942. D. S. A. No. 1088.
126. B. 1277. H Tobiesen, Esq.
127. Vejle hall-mark (B. 2922) and B. 2931. V. Steensen-Leth, Esq. Steensgaard.
128. B. 2276. P. Wedel-Heinen, Esq., Elvedgaard.
129. B. 1808. H. Drucker, Esq.
130. KM 1747 and B. 409. Mrs. Birte Hansen.
131. Aalborg hall-mark 1745 and B. 2404. J. Kjølbye, Esq., Kolding.
132. B. 2735. D. S. A. Nos. 384—385.
133. KM 1747 and B. 444. Messrs. Berg Bros.
134. KM 1760 and master's mark IBS (cf. B. page 71; the mark is not illustrated). D. S. A. No. 501.
135. B. 1289. H. Drucker, Esq.
136. B. 1873. J. Unsgaard, Esq. Mit b. ku. No. 374.
137. B. 1205. Messrs. Berg Bros.
138. KM 1757 and B. 449. Erik Lassen: Sølvtøj (in C. L. Davids Samling. Nogle Studier. 1948), p. 170.
139. KM 1762 and B. 495.
140. KM 1777 and B. 623. H. Drucker, Esq.
141. KM 1781 and 649.
142. KM 1781 and B. 615. Count Wedell, Wedellsborg.
143. KM 1789. Master's mark illegible.
144. KM (the date illegible) and B. 704. Dansk kunsth. No. 88. London No. 377.
145. KM 1806 and B. 740.
146. KM 1807 and B. 613. Mus. No. 174/1922.
147. KM 1812 and B. 779. Peter Koch, Esq.
148. Sønderborg hall-mark and B. 2751. B. Reimuth, Esq.
149. KM 1843 and B. 1062. P. U. Michelsen, Esq. Erik Lassen and Ole Wanscher: A. Michelsen og dansk Sølvsmedekunst, 1941, pp. 19, 74, 75. Dansk kunsth. No. 90. London No. 381.

150. KM 1786 and B. 498. The stand: KM 1773; master's mark illegible. The lamp: B. 797.
151. B. 2288.
152. KM 1772 and B. 375. H. Drucker, Esq.
153. KM 1835 and B. 964. Baroness Esther Rosenkrantz.
154. B. 1805. Mus. No. 90, 39.
155. KM 1806 and B. 740.
156. KM 1813 and B. 829. Count Wedell, Wedellsborg.
157. KM 1739 and B. 330. Baron A. G. T. Reedtz-Thott, Gavnø. D. S. A. No. 390.
158. KM 1739 and B. 354. The feet: B. 738.
159. B. 1805.
160. KM 1762 and B. 481.
161. KM 1769 and master's mark IIS (cf. B. page 76; the mark is not illustrated). H. Drucker, Esq. Dansk kunsth. No. 74.
162. B. 1288. D. S. A. No. 562.
163. KM 1753 and B. 410.
164. KM 176.. (the last figure and the master's mark illegible). London No. 367.
165. KM 1768 and B. 376 (with the date 1768). Baroness Esther Rosenkrantz.
166. KM 1776 and B. 497. Count W. Knuth, Egeløkke. Cf. Erik Lassen: Sølvtøj (in C. L. Davids Samling. Nogle Studier. 1948), pp. 145 and 147.
167. KM 1788 and B. 528. C. G. A. Fenger, Esq. D. S. A. No. 734. Mit b. ku. No. 381.
168. B. 528. Formerly in the Ole Olsen Collection.
169. KM 1790 and B. 616.
170. KM 1798 and B. 596.
171. KM 1806 and B. 740.
172. KM 1832. Master's mark illegible (probably B. 833). Mrs. Mathilde v. Haffner.
173. KM 1811 and B. 829.
174. KM 1701 and B. 280. Messrs. Berg Bros.
175. KM 1701 and B. 280. Messrs. Berg Bros. Dansk kunsth. No. 53.
176. KM 1729 and B. 264. H. Drucker, Esq.
177. KM 1729 and B. 264. H. Drucker, Esq.
178. KM 1737 and B. 324.
179. KM 1742 and B. 407. Messrs. Berg Bros.
180. KM 1733 and B. 351. Mus. Cat. 1943 No. 3662, 14.
181. KM 1729 and B. 331. H. Drucker, Esq.
182. B. 1805. H. Drucker, Esq.
183. B. 2410. Tage Hansen, Esq.
184. B. 1287. H. Tobiesen, Esq.
185. KM 1757 and B. 505. Mrs. Carl Oppen.
186. B. 2499.
187. B. 1284. H. Drucker, Esq.
188. B. 1288. D. S. A. No. 565.
189. B. 2738. Joachim Giersing, Esq.
190. KM 1778 and B. 527 (with the date 78).
191. KM 1790 and B. 616.
192. KM 1762 and B. 495.
193. KM 1806 and B. 742.
194. B. 910.
195. KM 1817 and B. 767.
196. Tønder hall-mark and B. 2858. Mus. No. 326/1931.
197. KM 1813 and B. 829. D. S. A. No. 907.
198. B. 871. D. S. A. No. 938.
199. KM 1797 and B. 716. Mus. No. 178/1922.
200. B. 1396. Baroness Esther Rosenkrantz.
201. KM 1701 and B. 280. Messrs. Berg Bros.

202. KM 1740 and B. 368.
203. KM 1752 and B. 372. Messrs. Berg Bros.
204. KM 1762 and B. 495.
205. Viborg hall-mark (B. 2970) and B. 2980. Messrs. Berg Bros. Dansk kunsth. No. 50.
206. B. 226. A. G. T. Reedtz-Thott, Gavnø. D. S. A. No. 146.
207. KM 1707 and B. 297 (with the date 1706). H. Drucker, Esq.
208. Odense hall-mark 1689 and B. 2257. Hj. Bruhn, Esq.
209. KM 1719 and B. 323. H. Tobiesen, Esq.
210. B. 2276. H. Tobiesen, Esq.
211. KM 1728 and B. 321 with the date 172(1?).
212. KM 1742 and B. 397. Nyrop fig. 50. Dansk kunsth. No. 63.
213. KM 1725 and B. 339.
214. KM 1750 and B. 372. H. Drucker, Esq.
215. B. 2418. H. Drucker, Esq.
216. KM 1723 and B. 340.
217. B. 2685. J. Kjølbye, Esq., Kolding.
218. B. 2935. J. Kjølbye, Esq., Kolding.
219. KM 1755 and B. 373. H. Tobiesen, Esq.
220. B. 566 and B. page 254. H. Tobiesen, Esq.
221. B. 1389 (no marks on the oil- and vinegar-jugs). V. Strøyberg, Esq.
222. B. 2415 (on the mustard-pot and the spoon: B. 913). Dansk kunsth. No. 76.
223. B. 1287. Mrs. Carl Oppen.
224. B. 1287. H. Drucker, Esq.
225. B. 509 or 510.
226. KM 1788 and B. 688.
227. B. 1289.
228. KM 1776 and B. 586. H. Drucker, Esq.
229. B. 2274.
230. B. 1270. D. S. A. No. 217.
231. B. 1783. H. Tobiesen, Esq.
232. KM 1778 and B. 610.
233. B. 498. H. Drucker, Esq.
234. KM 1788 and master's mark C H (cf. B. page 93; the mark is not illustrated).
235. KM 1788 and B. 688. The spoon: B. 682.
236. B. 2422. John Hagemann, Esq.
237. B. 1822.
238. B. 1822.
239. Svendborg hall-mark and B. 2695.
240. KM 1805 and B. 757.
241. B. 900.
242. B. 596.
243. KM (the date is illegible) and B. 752.
244. B. 2943.
245. KM 1843 and master's mark C P (the mark is not illustrated by Bøje).
246. KM 1828 and B. 851. Mus. No. B. 2/1913.
247. B. 1280. H. Drucker, Esq.
248. KM 1733 and B. 324. Mrs. Carl Oppen.
249. KM 1742 and B. 397. Mus. Cat. 1943 No. 3305, 22.
250. KM 1775 and B. 605.
251. KM 174.. (the last figure is illegible) and B. 437.
252. KM 1769 and B. 495. H. Drucker, Esq.
253. KM 1747 and B. 361.
254. KM 1761 and B. 417.
255. KM 1762 and B. 491. Mus. Cat. 1943 No. 3305, 23.

256. B. 675. Mrs. Carl Oppen.
257. B. 784 and the mark of the royal surveyor (the »guardein«) F. Fabritius (died 1823). Mus. No. B. 9/1913.
258. Tønder hall-mark and B. 2871. Mus. No. A. 11/1932.
259. KM 1815 and B. 913. Mus. No. A. 41/1914.
260. KM 1812 and B. 850.
261. KM 1812 and B. 884. H. Tobiesen, Esq.
262. B. 2257. H. Tobiesen, Esq.
263. KM 1701 and B. 281. Messrs. Berg Bros.
264. KM 1719 and B. 328.
265. KM 1725 and B. 264.
266. B. 2276. P. Wedel-Heinen, Esq., Elvedgaard.
267. B. 1487 (the identification of this mark by Bøje is wrong; cf. B. page 195). Hj. Bruhn, Esq.
268. KM 1733 and B. 368.
269. KM 1745 and B. 407. Messrs. Berg Bros.
270. KM 174.. (the last figure is illegible) and B. 420. Hj. Bruhn, Esq.
271. KM 1732 and B. 345.
272. B. 410 (with the date 1754). Mrs. Else Oluf Thomsen.
273. KM 1758 and B. 481. H. Drucker, Esq.
274. B. 1783. Mrs. Carl Oppen.
275. KM 1768 and B. 564. Mrs. Carl Oppen.
276. KM 1772 and B. 527.
277. B. 2415. Mrs. Carl Oppen.
278. B. 1288. D. S. A. No. 563.
279. B. 1288. D. S. A. No. 564.
280. KM 1773 and master's mark B I (cf. B. page 85; the mark is not illustrated). H. Drucker, Esq.
281. KM 1761 or 62 and B. 495.
282. B. 605. H. Drucker, Esq.
283. KM 1776 and B. 534. H. Tobiesen, Esq.
284. B. page 245 (the mark is not illustrated).
285. KM 1786 and B. 498 (with the date 86). Count L. Moltke-Huitfeldt, Glorup.
286. KM 1777 and B. 623. D. S. A. No. 675. Dansk kunsth. No. 77.
287. B. 584. D. S. A. No. 736.
288. KM 1778. The master's mark is illegible.
289. B. 1822. Mus. No. 177/1922.
290. Odense hall-mark (B. 2239) and B. 2313. Hj. Bruhn, Esq.
291. KM 1812 and B. 883. Leif Ørting Jacobsen, Esq.
292. KM 1810 and B. 742. H. Tobiesen, Esq.
293. KM 1807 and B. 742. Count L. Moltke-Huitfeldt, Glorup.
294. KM 1813. The master's mark is illegible. Count L. Moltke-Huitfeldt, Glorup.
295. KM 1823 and B. 662. Formerly in the collection of Count F. Brockenhuus-Schack.
296. KM 1814 and B. 2622. Count Wedell, Wedellsborg.
297. KM 1832 and B. 1004. D. S. A. No. 1099.
298. B. 447. D. S. A. No. 449.
299. B. 508 (with the date 1759). Baron A. G. T. Reedtz-Thott, Gavnø. D. S. A. No. 499.
300. KM 1740 and B. 341. H. Drucker, Esq.
301. KM 1731 and B. 362. H. Drucker, Esq.
302. Aabenraa hall-mark. The master's mark is illegible. J. Kjølbye, Esq., Kolding.

303. Tønder hall-mark and B. 2864. J. Kjølbye, Esq., Kolding.
304. KM 1779 and B. 543.
305. B. 1354. H. v. Haffner, Esq.
306. B. 1290.
307. Odense hall-mark and B. 2295.
308. KM 1784 and B. 528.
309. B. 1255 .
310. Næstved hall-mark for 1608 and B. 3059. D. og S. page 67, No. 19.
311. B. 1904.
312. The master's mark is illegible. Mit b. Ku. No. 356.
313. KM 1608 and B. 136. H. Drucker, Esq. D. S. A. No. 7. E. Hannover: Pottery and porcelain (1925). II, 1, fig. 127. Dansk kunsth. No. 28.
314. Master's mark B. (unidentified). D. og S. page 129 (Ribe amt No. 2). Mus. No. 12537.
315. B. 2929 (this is in effect the master's mark of Hans Olufsen — mentioned B. page 426).
316. B. 1272. Mrs. Else Oluf Thomsen.
317. B. 1258. Hj. Bruhn, Esq. H. Schmitz No. 458.
318. Master's mark D (unidentified). Hj. Bruhn, Esq. H. Schmitz No. 432.
319. B. 2264. H. Tobiesen, Esq.
320. B. 2496. Tage Hansen, Esq.
321. KM 1687 and B. 183. D. S. A. No. 117. Dansk kunsth. No. 49.
322. Odense hall-mark (B. 2235) and B. 2267.
323. KM 1716 and B. 321. Count L. Moltke-Huitfeldt, Glorup.
324. Odense hall-mark and B. 2270. J. Swane, Esq., Vejle.
325. KM 1718 and B. 328.
326. KM 1734 and B. 351.
327. KM 1732 and B. 353. Mus. Cat. 1943 Nos. 3305, 15—16.
328. KM 1733 and B. 345. Tage Hansen, Esq.
329. KM 1756 and B. 374. H. Tobiesen, Esq.
330. KM 17 ... (the last two figures are illegible) and the mark of the royal surveyor (»guardein«) Conrad Ludolf (1679—1729); the master's mark is illegible. Count Wedell, Wedellsborg.
331. KM 1733 and B. 368.
332. KM 1737 and B. 330 (with the date 1737).
333. The bowl: KM 1741 and B. 349. The dish: KM 1750 and B. 449.
334. B. 1805.
335. KM 1745 and B. 385. Mit b. ku. No. 371.
336. B. 1208. Mus. Cat. 1943 No. 3303, 6.
337. KM 1762 and B. 410 (with the date 1758).
338. B. 2410. H. Tobiesen, Esq.
339. KM 1792 and B. 742.
340. B. 2316. V. Steensen-Leth, Esq., Steensgaard.
341. The tureen: KM 1754 and B. 444. The dish: KM 1770 and B. 376 (with the date 1770). Countess Fanny Rantzau, Krengerup.
342. KM 1777 and B. 534 (with the date 77). Count L. Moltke-Huitfeldt, Glorup.
343. KM 1799 and B. 778. Mus. Cat. 1943 No. 5222.
344. Odense hall-mark and B. 2313 with the date 98.
345. KM 1829 and master's mark N C, cf. B. page 108; the mark is not illustrated). Mus. Cat. 1943 No. 6168.

346. KM 1801 and B. 753. H. Tobiesen, Esq.
347. KM 1844 and B. 964. C. G. R. Fenger, Esq.
348. KM 1777 and B. 534 (with the date 77). Count L. Moltke-Huitfeldt, Glorup.
349. KM 1766 and B. 375. Countess Fanny Rantzau, Krengerup.
350. KM 1774 and B. 532. Count Wedell, Wedellsborg.
351. KM 1788 and B. 616 (with the date 87). Mrs. Carl Oppen.
352. B. 613 and B. 616 (with the date 87).
353. KM 1806 and B. 765. Mrs. Else Oluf Thomsen.
354. KM 1829 and B. 767. Mus. Cat. 1943 No. 6169.
355. KM 1740 and B. 361. Mrs. Else Oluf Thomsen.
356. KM 1742 and B. 407.
357. KM 1742 and B. 407.
358. KM 1744 and B. 397. Mrs. Else Oluf Thomsen.
359. B. 1282. Mrs. Olsen, Hasseris.
360. KM 1750 and B. 409. Mrs. Else Oluf Thomsen.
361. KM 1752 and B. 420.
362. KM 1755 and B. 422.
363. KM 1760 and B. 410. H. Drucker, Esq.
364. B. 1516. H. Drucker, Esq.
365. KM 1780 and B. 588. Mus. Cat. 1943 No. 3661—62, 7.
366. KM 1770 and B. 458 (with the date 1770).
367. KM 1774 and B. 411. H. Tobiesen, Esq.
368. B. 509 (with the date 1776).
369. KM 177.. (the last figure is illegible) and B. 532 (with the date 1771).
370. KM 1826 and B. 2622.
371. KM 1821 and B. 833.
372. The warming-dish: KM (the date is illegible) and B. 443. The lamp: B. 616.
373. No marks.
374. Master's mark I S (cf. B. pages 25—26; the mark is not illustrated).
375. KM 1689 and B. 221 (with the date 1688).
376. KM 1701 and B. 280. Mus. No. 97 — 1894.
377. KM 1703 and B. 284. H. H. Bruun, Esq.
378. B. 1798. H. Drucker, Esq.
379. KM 1741 and B. 385. H. Tobiesen, Esq.
380. KM 1829 and a master's mark very like B. 767. Mus. Cat. 1943 No. 3305, 17.
381. KM 1766 and B. 511. Mus. Cat. 1943 No. 3303[13].
382. B. 1798. Mus. Cat. 1943 No. 3305[33].
383. KM 1722 and B. 304. Mrs. Carl Oppen.
384. KM 1742 and B. 399. Messrs. Berg Bros.
385. KM 1767 and B. 511.
386. KM 1740 and B. 336. H. Tobiesen, Esq.
387. KM 1750 and B. 447. H. Drucker, Esq.
388. The dish: KM 1741 and B. 354 (with the date 1740); the lid: KM 1742 and the same master's mark as on the dish.
389. B. 1373. Messrs. Berg Bros.
390. KM 1745 and B. 419.
391. KM 1755 and B. 373. Messrs. Berg Bros.
392. KM 1769 and B. 508. H. Tobiesen, Esq.
393. KM 1770 and B. 508 (with the date 1770).
394. KM 1767 and B. 375.
395. KM 1758 and master's mark G H (cf. B. page 75; the mark is not illustrated). Mrs. Carl Oppen. Dansk kunsth. No. 69.
396. KM 1796 and B. 544.

397. KM 1792 and B. 498. H. Drucker, Esq.
398. KM (the date is illegible) and B. 765.
399. KM 1814 and B. 836.
400. KM 1815 and an illegible master's mark.
401. No marks. D. og S. page 88 No. 9. Mus. No. 15624.
402. No marks. D. og S. page 91 No. 24. Mus. No. 10701.
403. The marks are unidentified. D. og S. page 92 No. 25.
404. No marks. D. og S. page 87 No. 1. Mus. No. 21457.
405. No marks. D. og S. page 87 No. 2. Mus. No. 22179.
406. KM 1623 and B. 148. D. og S. page 99 No. 48.
407. B. 150. D. og S. page 101 No. 65. Mus. No. 20668.
408. KM 1623 and an illegible master's mark. D. og S. page 98 No. 40. Mus. No. D. 3044.
409. B. 143. D. og S. page 99 No. 52. Mus. No. 10081.
410. No marks. D. og S. page 94 No. 8. Mus. No. D. 4905.
411. No marks. D. og S. page 92 No. 1. Mus. No. 10705.
412. Odense hall-mark and B. 2262. D. og S. page 136 No. 1. Mus. No. D. 2479.
413. The master's mark is illegible. Mus. No. 10805.
414. B. 2169. Mus. No. 8067.
415. No marks. D. og S. page 118 No. 4. Mus. No. D. 642.
416. B. 1904. D. og S. page 121 No. 1. Mus. No. 16081.
417. No marks. D. og S. page 117. Mus. No. D. 641.
418. No marks.
419. No marks.
420. No marks. Dansk kunsth. No. 36.
421. No marks.
422. a) No marks. b) A master's mark, not illustrated by Bøje (cf. B. page 35). — Baron A. G. T. Reedtz-Thott, Gavnø. D. S. A. Nos. 48—49.
423. KM 1654 and B. 177. Mus. No. 28/1900.
424. KM 1698 and B. 246. Mus. No. 4/1910.
425. KM 1663 and B. 169. Mus. No. 103/1894.
426. Næstved hall-mark and B. 2174. Mrs. Else Oluf Thomsen.
427. B. 1261. Mrs. Else Oluf Thomsen.
428. KM 1725 and master's mark BL (cf. B. page 55; the mark is not illustrated). Mrs. Else Oluf Thomsen.
429. No marks. Dansk kunsth. No. 40.
430. No marks. Dansk kunsth. No. 41.
431. No marks.
432. No marks.
433. No marks.
434. Odense hall-mark for 1699 (B. 2236) and B. 2267.
435. KM 1721 and B. 304.
436. Nakskov hall-mark (B. 2037), the date 1699 and B. 2042. Hj. Bruhn, Esq.
437. B. 600.
438. B. 1372.
439. B. 572.
440. B. 1389.
441. B. 425.
442. B. 362.
443. B. 431. Mrs. Carl Oppen.
444. B. 1805. Mrs. Carl Oppen.
445. KM 1730 and B. 340. Mrs. Carl Oppen.
446. KM 1791 and B. 665. Mrs. Birte Hansen.

447. Kalundborg hall-mark for 1758 and B. 1873. Mrs. Birte Hansen.
448. KM 1759. The master's mark is illegible.
449. B. 537 (with the date 77).
450. KM 1768 and B. 457.
451. KM 1783 and B. 660.
452. KM 1769 and B. 410. H. Tobiesen, Esq.
453. KM 1772 and B. 1681. H. Tobiesen, Esq.
454. KM 1786 and B. 689. H. Tobiesen, Esq.
455. The knife: KM 1745 and B. 409; the fork: KM 1757 and B. 449. Mus. Cat. 1943 No. 3305[12].
456. KM 1758; the master's mark is illegible.
457. KM 174 (4?) and B. 399. Mus. Cat. 1943 No. 3305[13].
458. B. 540. H. Drucker, Esq.
459. KM 1738 and B. 315.
460. KM 1772 and B. 413.
461. KM 1785 and B. 610.
462. KM 1753 and B. 409. Mrs. Birte Hansen.
463. KM 1760 and B. 374.
464. KM 1788 and B. 600 (with the date 87).
465. KM 1754 and B. 472 (with the date 1752).
466. KM 1754 and B. 472 (with the date 1752).
467. KM 1753 and B. 334.
468. Aabenraa hall-mark and B. 1203. J. Kjølbye, Esq., Kolding.
469. Ribe hall-mark and B. 2478. J. Kjølbye, Esq., Kolding.
470. Tønder hall-mark and B. 2866. J. Kjølbye, Esq., Kolding.
471. Aabenraa hall-mark and B. 1214.
472. Aabenraa hall-mark and B. 1219.
473. KM 1837 and B. 805.
474. B. 620.
475. KM 1823 and B. 801.
476. KM 1724 and B. 304. Mrs. Carl Oppen.
477. B. 372. Mrs. Carl Oppen.
478. B. 1215.
479. B. 663.
480. B. 1388.
481. B. 2611.
482. KM 1785 and B. 2212.
483. Aabenraa hall-mark and B. 1219.
484. B. 2418.
485. Odense hall-mark and B. 2296. Mrs. M. Westergaard, Hillerød. D. S. A. No. 515.
486. KM 182 .. (the last figure and the master's mark are illegible). Mus. No. 1673.
487. KM 1763 and B. 539.
488. KM 1779 and B. 531. Mrs. Carl Oppen.
489. KM 1783 and B. 654. Mus. Cat. 1943 No. 3305[11].
490. KM 1805 and B. 784. Mus. No. 592/1928.
491. B. 434. H. Drucker, Esq.
492. B. 2415. H. Drucker, Esq.
493. B. 600 (with the date 81). H. Drucker, Esq.
494. Aabenraa hall-mark and B. 1217. J. Kjølbye, Esq., Kolding.
495. B. 1590. J. Kjølbye, Esq., Kolding.
496. B. 1596. J. Kjølbye, Esq., Kolding.

INDEX TO NAMES OF GOLDSMITHS
WHOSE WORK IS ILLUSTRATED IN THIS BOOK

The figures refer to the numbers of the texts accompanying the pictures.
When names are given without the town of origin, this is to be read as Copenhagen.

1 a. »Rose Blossom«. Large silver-gilt drinking vessel, with two handles and loose lid, resting on three lions and three pomegranates. Relief, cast and engraved with hunting scenes in Renaissance style. Engraved verse: »Mit navn det kaldes en Rosenblomme« (»My name is called Rose Blossom« etc.). Cartouches with coats of arms of the Skovgaard and Parsberg families and inscription in relief: HANS SKOVGAARD — ANNE PARSBERG 1577. Probably a christening present from Hans Skovgaard, Privy Councillor, and his wife to Christian IV in 1577. Made by Acgidius Loidt, Copenhagen. Height 37.5 cms. Danish National Museum.

1 b. Lid of »Rose Blossom« (See previous side).

2 b. Lid of tankard No. 2 a. Reproduced full size, as is also the tankard itself (opposite). On the other hand the lid above is reproduced on the same scale as »Rose Blossom« (No. 1 a.), i. e. about one-third full size.

2 a. Tankard, silver parcel-gilt. Moulded base. Thumb-piece in form of an hour-glass with death's head. Side completely covered with engraved animals, plants and four cartouches with the elements: AER, AQVA, TERRA, IGNIS. On the lid are engraved symbols and inscriptions relating to death: SIC TRANSIT GLORIA MUNDI, MEMORARE NOVISSIMA ECCE and also GLED DIG ICK DERAF AT DIEN FIEND DØER TI AT VI SKULLE ALLE DØ (»Rejoice not that thine enemy dieth, for we shall all die«). Over the rim of the base is engraved a Greek inscription: «*Ο ΠΟΛΛΑ ΠΙΝΩΝ ΠΟΛΛΑΚ ΕΞΑΜΑΡΤΑ-NEI*« (»He who drinks much sins often«). On the handle is engraved: SITIS SOBRII AD PRECATIONEM 1. PET. 4. and date 1569. The typical tankard of the Danish Renaissance during the period from the middle of the 16th to the middle of the 17th century is, like this one, cylindrical and comparatively tall (it is often taller than this); it has a moulded lid and stands on a moulded and projecting base; often a ring engirdles the lower part of the tankard. Undoubtedly Danish work, by an unknown goldsmith ca. 1569. Height 14.0 cms.

Privately owned.

3. Silver-gilt tankard. On the lid are the coat of arms of Frederik Hobe and his wife Sidsel Urne and their initials in relief. Engraved Renaissance ornament and (added later) a cartouche with an inscription stating that the tankard was presented to Nysted Church in 1593. Probably the tankard was originally made for secular use. Made by an unknown Danish goldsmith shortly before 1593. Height 16.6 cms.   Danish National Museum.

4. Tankard with engraved and chased Renaissance ornament. Made by an unknown, presumably Copenhagen goldsmith shortly after 1600. Height 22.6 cms.
      Danish National Museum.

5. Silver-mounted glass jug. On the glass are engraved the initials, and painted the coat of arms, of King Christian IV and Queen Anna Catherine; on the silver lid are engraved the coat of arms and initials of Lord Lieutenant Ebbe Munk and his wife. On Renaissance tankards a pear-shaped thumb-piece is found nearly as often as a flat thumb-piece with figures cast in relief. Height (without lid) 13.0 cms.   Danish National Museum.

6. Silver-gilt tankard. Engraved Renaissance ornament surrounding representations of the seven liberal arts (after a French ornament engraving by Etienne Delaune, died 1583) and Danish and Latin maxims. Made by an unknown Odense goldsmith at the close of the 16th Century. Height 21.5 cms.   Privately owned.

7. Silver-gilt tankard with engraved Renaissance ornament. On the lid are chased the coat of arms and initials
of Jørgen Brahe, Privy Councillor (died 1661) and his
wife Anna Gyldenstjerne. Presumably made by Daniel
Harder, Odense, in the 1620's. Height 20.7 cms.
                              Nordiska Museet, Stockholm.

8. Silver-gilt tankard resting on three lions séjant. Three
oval medallions depicting men's heads, surrounded by fruit
and flower ornaments, all in chased work. The tankard
reveals German influence and is of a type unusual in Denmark. Made by Steen Pedersen, Copenhagen, 1639. Height
16.8 cms.   Privately owned.

9. Tankard with chased diamond bosses on the base and
lid and twisted ring with cherubs' heads; engraved orna-
ments surrounding representations of Justice, Godliness and
Love. In the lid is inset a silver-gilt wedding medallion.
Made by Ove Nielsen, Aarhus, presumably in the 1620's.
Height 22.5 cms.   Danish National Museum.

10. Tankard, plain, rather lower than those shown before. The lid is slightly domed (cf. No. 14). On the lid
a garland of fruits is engraved around a shield with the
owner's initials and an IHS monogram together with the
date 1646. Thumb-piece shaped like a pine cone. Made by
Hans Olufsen, Vejle. Height 13.5 cms.
Danish National Museum.

11. Tankard. The side is engraved with Renaissance ornament, the lid with the owner's initials and the date 1673.
Along the edge of the lid is engraved: »TIL GUD MIDT
HAAB ALLENE« (»In God alone my hope«). The tankard
was probably made thirty to forty years before the date
was added. Presumably made by Mads Bertelsen, Kolding.
Height 15.7 cms.   Danish National Museum.

12. Tankard resting on three lion heads. Around the foot
is chased a lozengy band. On the side opposite the handle
are engraved two lions with a shield bearing the initials of
the owner, a commoner. On the lid is a German medallion
dating from 1621. Made by Albert Carstensen, Copenhagen, presumably about 1640—1650. Height 13.5 cms.
Frederiksborg.

13. Tankard, plain, of the lower type (cf. No. 10) that became general towards the middle of the century. In the centre of the lid are engraved the Ulfeldt coat of arms and the name KNUD ULFELDT 1644. Made by Hans Krey, Odense. Height 16.5 cms.

Privately owned.

14. Tankard, silver parcel-gilt. With its very low body and its slightly domed lid the tankard belongs to the period of transition towards Baroque. It is covered with engravings; on the side are pictures showing the story of Lucretia, on the lid a leaf decoration surrounds Kirsten Munk's coat of arms and her initials with the year 1653. (Kirsten Munk was the morganatic wife of King Christian IV). Made by Daniel Harder, Odense. Height 9.0 cms.

Rosenborg.

15 a. Tankard, plain, resting on three pomegranates. On the lid an engraved chaplet of flowers surrounds a coat of arms and initials, showing that the tankard has belonged to Claus Gagge of Drageholm and his wife Sophie Pors of Skovsgaard. The date 1648 is also engraved. Feet cast in the shape of pomegranates with leaves soldered to the tankard became typical of Danish Baroque tankards from about the middle of the century: generally, as in this case, found together with a thumb-piece consisting of two small pomegranates. Made by Niels Enevoldsen, Copenhagen. Height 20.0 cms.

Privately owned.

15 b. Lid to above tankard.

16 a. Tankard, plain, resting on three pomegranates. On the lid are engraved monograms of the owners, who are commoners, and the date 1655 surrounded by an ornament in the »auricular« style (frequently met with in early Scandinavian Baroque but seldom seen on silverware), and a wreath of flowers. As in the Renaissance period, there is not much difference in the older Baroque between the work of goldsmiths of Copenhagen and those of the provincial towns. (Cf. Nos. 15 and 16). Height 14.3 cms. Privately owned.

(Auricular Style: Fr. »style auriculaire«, German »Ohrmuschelstil«, Danish »Bruskbarok«. A type of Baroque ornament employing exuberant lines and grotesque masks, and occasionally a motif based on the outline of the human ear. The style is found mainly in Germany and Scandinavia c. 1630—1660).

16 b. Lid to above tankard.

17 a. Tankard, resting on three pomegranates. It is in the same form as the one preceding, but the sides and lid are fully decorated with chased Baroque flowers, which are of general occurrence in the last third of the 17th Century but are seldom, as here (following a German pattern) seen covering the whole surface. On the lid is a mask cartouche with monograms of the owners, who are commoners, and the date 1668. Made by Dionis Willadsen, Næstved. Height 19.2 cms.

Privately owned.

17 b. Lid to above tankard.

18. Tankard, plain, resting on three lions séjant. On the lid an engraved garland of flowers surrounds the coat-of-arms of an English noble family. Lions séjant with their forepaws resting on a ball are often used, as in this case, for the feet of a Baroque tankard as an alternative to pomegranates; as a rule the thumb-piece is cast in the same form. Made by Jørgen Stilche, Copenhagen, 1671. Height 21.5 cms.   Privately owned.

19. Tankard, resting on three lions séjant. Shape as in previous illustration, but the tankard is completely covered with chased human, animal and plant motifs. In the centre of the lid is a silver-gilt panel with a coat of arms indicating that the owners are commoners and the legend: PETER JESSEN and MARIE KEGGE-BENS 1669. Made by Carsten Lauridsen, Copenhagen. Height 21.5 cms.

Danish National Museum.

20. Tankard, plain, resting on three pomegranates. The thumb-piece is a lion lying transversely, not often seen in Denmark. On the lid, leaf-work is engraved around a coat of arms and the owners' monograms NBS. CB. together with the date 1680. On the side a cypher, repeated and reversed has been engraved at a later date. Made by Joen Andersen, Helsingør, ca. 1680. Height 21.5 cms.   Victoria & Albert Museum, London.

21. Tankard, resting on three pomegranates. Thumb-piece in the shape of a lion. Chased flowers on the lid, over the feet and around the upper end of the handle. Engraved garland of flowers, with owner's initials and the date 1687. On the lid a silver-gilt German medallion. Made by Mikkel Jensen, Aalborg, 1686. Height 16.0 cms. Danish National Museum.

22. Tankard, plain, resting on three sitting dogs. Flowers are boldly chased over the feet and on the lid. In the latter part of the 17th Century, tankards were generally plain with chased ornaments on the lid and over the feet. The use of dogs for feet or thumb-piece was exceptional. In the lid is inset a silver-gilt wedding medallion. Made by Henrik Cortsen Holzkamph, Viborg, ca. 1700. Height 25.0 cms.

Privately owned.

23. Tankard, plain, resting on three lions séjant. Above the feet are chased acanthus leaves;
on the lid, chased flowers and birds surround
a name-plate with cypher, repeated and reversed
and the date 1717. Made by Mogens Thommesen Løwenhertz, Horsens. One of the biggest
Danish silver tankards still existing. Height
25.5 cms.   Danish National Museum.

24. Tankard, plain, resting on three lions séjant. On the side are engraved the initials of
the owner, a commoner, and the date 1722.
Chased acanthus leaves over the feet and on the
lid, surrounding a medallion. Made by Mikkel
Jensen, Aalborg. Height 18.5 cms.
                         Odense Museum.

25. Lid of jug (stone jug or similar). On the lid a border chased with oblique radial gadrooning surrounds a German wedding medallion. Chased gadrooning is generally used in late Baroque. Made by Lorentz Nielsen, Copenhagen, 1722.   Privately owned.

26. Lid of tankard (the tankard is not reproduced here). Around the circumference of the lid is a rim of chased acanthus leaves and birds (a favourite motif of the goldsmith Mogens Löwenhertz — cf. No. 23) on a pounced background. In the centre is set a religious medallion surrounding which is engraved JOH. WILH. RIES 1722. Made by Mogens Thommesen Løwenhertz, Horsens. Diameter 15.5 cms.

Privately owned.

27 a. Tankard, plain, resting on three ball-and-claw feet. Above the feet is chased a representation of two children holding a heart (probably a motif peculiar to East Jutland). On the lid a chaplet of acanthus leaves surrounds the coat of arms of Count Christian Friis and the date 1722. Made by Zønnik Hansen Buxlund, Aarhus. Height 21.2 cms.

Privately owned.

27 b. Lid of above tankard.

28 b. Lid of tankard No. 28 a. Chased leaf-band border surrounds an inset wedding medallion. The rim is gadrooned (an ornament often present from the end of the 17th Century).

28 a. Tankard, resting on three ball-and-claw feet. On the side, chased and engraved ornaments in late Baroque style, with strapwork, masks, and cartouche with cypher NK repeated and reversed. Made by Laurids Holm, Aalborg, ca. 1730. Height 23 cm.   Privately owned.

29. Tankard, plain, resting on three ball-and-claw feet, the thumb-piece a lion. Over the feet and on the lid is engraved strapwork. In the lid is inset a silver gilt »speciedaler« (a Danish coin). Owner's initials and the date 1753 pricked in. Made by Johannes Zönnichsen Buxlund, Aarhus. Height 20.5 cms. »Den gamle By« (Old Town Museum), Aarhus.

30. Tankard, plain, resting on three lions séjant with balls, the thumb-piece a lion with shield. Engraved strapwork over the feet and on the lid surrounding an inset medallion. Made by Gert N. Thorbrügger, Kolding, ca. 1750. Height 19 cms.
Koldinghus Museum, Kolding.

31. (See opp., top left). Glass jug with silver lid. The lid is decorated with twisted fluting and contains an inset Danish Reformation medallion dated 1717. Thumb-piece a lion with shield, in which is a lime tree (no doubt the coat of arms of the burgher family Lindemann of Vejle). The lid rests on a glass jug of contemporary make engraved with the letters JLM (Johan Lindemann?). Made by Jørgen Nielsen Brosbøll, Vejle, 1756. Diam. 11 cms.
Privately owned.

32. (See opp., top right). Tankard, plain, resting on three lions séjant. Rococo leaves with stems engraved over the feet, in the cartouche at the side and on the lid surrounding a silver-gilt German medallion of about 1620. Made by Hans Budtz Sommerfeldt, Aalborg, ca. 1760—80. Height 20 cms.
Privately owned.

33. (See opp., below). Lid of faience jug. The rim is fluted and chased with rococo decoration. On the lid is inset a medallion made by G. W. Wahl to celebrate the official re-opening of Hirschholm Castle in 1744, with portrait of Queen Sophia Magdalena. Made by Troels Larsen Lund, Copenhagen, 1753. Diam. 11.3 cms.
Privately owned.

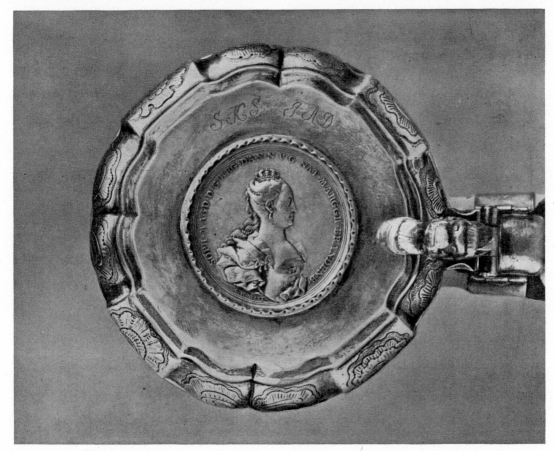

34. Goblet, with lid, chased gadrooning, engraved Renaissance tendrils with cherubs, and belt of leaf-work, thinly hammered in gothic style. Made by Anders Guldsmed, Køge, ca. 1550. Height (without lid) 24.3 cms.
                                                                                    Danish National Museum.

35. Beaker, with twisted ring adorned with cherubs, engraved Renaissance cartouche-work with the lion of Norway and shield bearing an owner's mark, the date 1589 and the initials K. R. D.; also an inscription EXPECTO LAETAM VICTORIAM SVB VEXILLO SALVATORIS. This is the oldest dated beaker of this form known in Denmark; it was the favourite form in Denmark during the Renaissance period. Made by Gabriel Brockmüller, Hillerød, ca. 1589. Height 12.3 cms.   Victoria and Albert Museum, London.

36. Beaker, plain, with spreading lip, engraved with Royal Danish coat-of-arms. From the shape of the beaker and the engraved coat-of-arms it would appear to belong to the middle of the 16th Century, but the maker's mark is that of an unknown Copenhagen master craftsman who lived about 1600. Height 16 cms.   Rosenborg.

37. Beaker, with lid, engraved with Renaissance ornaments and hunting-scenes, with inscription stating that the beaker was made from 30 silver coins which King Christian IV won in a drinking-match. It is called Christian IV's »Temperance Beaker«. Made by Gabriel Brockmüller, Hillerød, ca. 1600. Height 17 cms. Rosenborg.

38—39. Two goblets, with lid. Tongue-shaped gadrooning on foot and base, engraved ornament with birds, fruit clusters and shield with owner's mark M W and the date 1613. Silver-gilt on the inside. Made by Mads Claussøn, Copenhagen 1610. Given by the Mayor of Copenhagen, Mikkel Wibe, to the Danish Trading Gild along with two similar beakers (the four »Mayors' Beakers«). Height 25.8 cms.   Copenhagen Municipal Museum.

40. (Top left). Beaker, with twisted ring adorned with
cherubs. Engraved Renaissance ornament and shields with
initials. Made by unknown Danish goldsmith ca. 1600—
25. Height 13.8 cms.   Privately owned.

41. (Top right)) Beaker, with twisted ring adorned with
cherubs; underneath is a band with ornaments in relief;
above, Renaissance ornament, engraved with shield and
initials of owner. Letters ENDR engraved later. Made
by Carsten Tidemand, Odense, ca. 1625. Height 11.8
cms.   Privately owned.

42. (Bottom right). Beaker, shaped as in the preceding
illustration but with three notched rings with engraved
wave pattern; on the top and bottom rings are cherub
heads, the top one with lugs. Engraved ornaments and
initials of the owner. Made by Gievert Harder, Naestved
(master craftsman about 1686—1719). Degenerate forms
of this original Renaissance type of beaker appear well
on into the 18th Century; clearly a speciality of the
goldsmiths of Naestved. Height 13.6 cms.
          Privately owned.

43. Beaker of simple, slightly conical form with moulded base. Engraved animals dressed as Landsknechte, and above, the initials of the owner and the inscription: DRICKER. AF. MIG. GVD. IICKE. FORGETER. SAA. KAND. I. MED. LØST. BESE. DISE. KRIGSKNECTER. »Drink of me, and forget not God: so may you look upon these soldiers with pleasure«. Made by Johan Post or Jørgen Prytz, Copenhagen, ca. 1610—20. Height 10.1 cms.

Danish National Museum.

44. Beaker, with ornament of twisted rope around the middle. Moulded ring with lozengy ornament around base. Engraved fruit clusters, plant tendrils and masks, and owner's name. Unearthed at Askov in Jutland, having been buried during the Swedish war of 1658—59. Height 11 cms.

Danish National Museum.

45. Beaker, with spreading lip but no base; engraved Renaissance ornaments and shield with owner's mark. Unearthed at Braendekilde in Fyn, having been buried during the Swedish war of 1658—59. Height 9.7 cms.

Danish National Museum.

46. Beaker, hexagonal at the top, engraved with animals and shields with IHS monogram, owner's monogram and the date 1645. The lower part of the beaker is round and pounced. Made by Eiler Hansen Holm, Aalborg. Height 11 cms.   Privately owned.

47. Beaker, with spreading lip. The upper half is engraved with Renaissance ornament and the owner's name; the lower half gadrooned. The beaker is like No. 35 and Nos. 40—41 in form, with a foot like that of the Silver Rummers (Nos. 53—56). On the base is engraved the date 1640. Made by Albert Carstensen, Copenhagen. Height 11.1 cms.   Frederiksborg.

48. Gold beaker, plain; engraved with King Christian IV's monogram with crown and date 1644. Height 7 cms.   Rosenborg.

49. Beaker, octagonal, with moulded foot; engraved Renaissance ornament. Made probably by Lave Jørgensen, Horsens (master craftsman 1637—1652). Height 10.4 cms.
Danish National Museum.

50. Beaker, octagonal, engraved with owner's initials and the date 1639. Made by Christian Thommesen, Copenhagen. Height 8.3 cms. Danish National Museum.

51. Beaker, octagonal, with pounced sides and plain edges; panel engraved with owner's initials and the date 1640. Made by unknown Danish goldsmith. Height 9.7 cms.
Danish National Museum.

52. Beaker, hexagonal, engraved with large naturalistic flowers and owner's initials. Made by Hermand Jensen, Aalborg ca. 1660—70. Height 7.5 cms. Privately owned.

53. Cup, so-called Silver Rummer (Sølv Rømer) (old term for
this type of drinking cup with cylindrical foot and rounded
bowl). Richly engraved with hunting scenes and plant tendrils surrounding figures of monkeys playing musical instru-
ments, with escutcheon and initials showing that the cup
was made for a nobleman, Christen Harbo, and his wife
Birgitte Mund, probably for their wedding in 1595. Height
10.4 cms.   Danish National Museum.

54. Cup (Silver Rummer); engraved clusters of fruit, IHS
monogram and owner's initials. Made by Giert Hermandsen,
Aarhus (master craftsman 1613—42). Height 8 cms.
                                           Danish National Museum.

55. Cup (Silver Rummer); engraved fruit clusters and other
ornaments. Danish work from about 1625. Height 9.2 cms.
                                           Danish National Museum.

56. Cup (Silver Rummer); engraved Renaissance ornaments.
Made by unknown Danish goldsmith, ca. 1600—25. Height
7.9 cms.
        Kunstindustrimuseet (Museum of Applied Art), Oslo.

57. Beaker, gilt, cylindrical, with round bottom and three ball feet. Plain; engraved with coat-of-arms and initials of a nobleman, Corfits Rud, and his wife Birgitte Rosensparre, and the date 1631. Height 13 cms.

Danish National Museum.

58. Beaker, same form as No. 57, resting on three cast geese. Coins are inset in the beaker's plain side, an ornament often employed during the next hundred years (also on tankards). Made by Johan Thomsen Stichmann, Copenhagen, 1654. Height 15.5 cms.   Rosenborg.

59. Beaker, with lid, plain, flat-bottomed, resting on three pomegranates; finial likewise a pomegranate. On the side a chased olive-wreath surrounds the coat-of-arms and initials of Henrik Bielke, Lord High Admiral, and his wife Edel Ulfeld, with the date 1656. Made by Mathias Hielm, Copenhagen, 1654. Height 19.1 cms.

Danish National Museum.

60. Beaker, plain, resting on three pomegranates. On the side are engraved the coat of arms and initials of Børge Trolle, a nobleman (died 1676). Made by Mathias Silm, Copenhagen. Height 10.5 cms. Odense Museum.

61. Beaker, without foot. Pounced side, with a plain band around the top and bottom, and a laurel wreath engraved around the coat of arms and initials of Hans Lindenov, Privy Councillor, and his wife Lisbeth Sophie Rantzau, with the date 1645. Beakers of this shape and with similiar ornament were produced in large numbers from this period until late in the 18th Century. Made by Jørgen Stilche, Copenhagen, ca. 1645. Height 11.6 cms. Odense Museum.

62. Beaker with same form and decoration as No. 61; lid shaped as in No. 59, partly pounced. On the side is engraved a round panel with the initials of Miss Christence Brahe and her parents' coats of arms. Made by Hans Krey, Odense, ca. 1665. Height 12.4 cms.

Danish National Museum.

63. Beaker with same form and decoration as Nos. 61—62. On the side is a round panel, on which is engraved the coat of arms and initials of a nobleman, Arild Svave and his wife, Margrethe Beck with the date 1665. Made by unknown Danish goldsmith. Height 7.3 cms.   Frederiksborg.

64. Beaker, plain, silver-gilt. Made by Jacob Zachariesen Hofmand, Kalundborg. Height 6.5 cms.   Frederiksborg.

65. Beaker shaped like Nos. 61—63, with similiar pounced side, resting on three pomegranates with cast acanthus leaf soldered to the beaker (cf. No. 15). In the plain band at the top are engraved the owner's initials and the date 1671. Made by Hans Thuresen, Aalborg. Height 8 cms.
                                                   Privately owned.

66. Beaker with chased Baroque plant ornaments; on the
plain upper rim are engraved the owners' initials and date
1663. The beaker is a typical example of the florid Baroque
chased plant ornamentation that was becoming common at
this period, and reached its climax in the last decade of the
century (see No. 68). Made by Jens Jensen Brun, Aalborg.
Height 9.4 cms. Danish National Museum.

67. Beaker, the whole of the surface richly engraved with
flowers, animals and human beings. On the plain rim are
engraved the initials of the owner, a commoner, and his
wife, with the date 1672. Made by Gert Clausen, Viborg.
Height 10.1 cms. Danish National Museum.

68. Beaker, chased with heavy Baroque flowers and leaves.
Cf. No. 66. Made by Jørgen Bloch, Copenhagen 1698.
Height 11.4 cms. Privately owned.

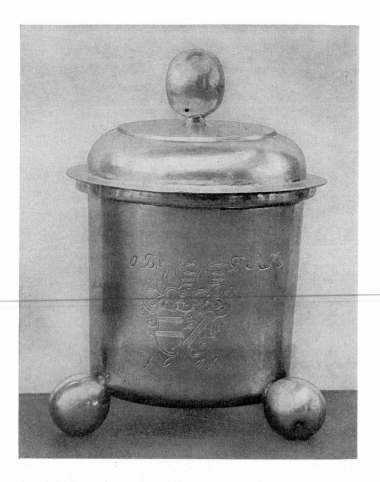

69. Beaker, plain, resting on three balls, with moulded lid and ball-shaped finial (cf. its shape with that of No. 59). On the side are engraved the coat of arms and initials of Otto Bielke of Sakslund and his wife Beate Rosenkrantz, with the date 1691. Made by unknown Danish goldsmith. Height 13.5 cms.   Privately owned.

70. Beaker, plain, low, resting on three pomegranates with symmetrical cast acanthus leaves; moulded lid with finial shaped like a pomegranate. Made by Isak Dubois, Copenhagen, 1688. Height 15 cms.   Privately owned.

71. Beaker with lid, same form as No. 69. On the side are two round panels with figures of small children (putti) surrounded by closely-chased acanthus leaf work, which covers the whole surface and also the lid. Around the rim of the beaker is a plain band engraved with the owner's initials and the date 1697. Made by Jacob Sørensen, Copenhagen 1696. Height 17 cms.   Kunstindustrimuseum (Museum of Applied Art), Oslo.

72. Beaker, resting on three balls; moulded lid with ball-shaped finial and wavy rim. Side and lid completely covered with acanthus leaves with outspread lobes on a pounced background. Around the rim of the beaker is a plain band engraved with the owners' initials. Made by Christen Jensen, Copenhagen 1705. Height 16 cms.   Privately owned.

73. Beaker, resting on three ball-and-claw feet. On the polished band around the mouth is engraved »Jørgen Arenfelt. Fru Ellen Christina Billau«, and on the side their coats of arms surrounded by acanthus leaves, all in chased work. Made by Johan H. Plumb, Aarhus, probably about 1690. Height 10.8 cms.   Frederiksborg.

74. Goblet with lid, silver parcel-gilt. Goblets, which were in general use until the end of the Renaissance, were only rarely — apart from Church and gild silverware — produced during the following centuries . . . . . Around the body of the vessel is fitted a cylindrical plate, chased with Cupids against a landscape background. On the base of the beaker and the lid is super-imposed a cast, reticulated band- and leaf-design over a gilt ground. On the lid is a cast Cupid. Made by Johan Heinrich Meel, Copenhagen 1692. Height 25.5 cms.   Rosenborg.

75. (See opp., top left). Beaker, plain, gilt inside. On the outside is engraved the coat of arms of the Benzon family with the insignia of the order of the Dannebrog (the most distinguished Danish order), probably referring to Niels Benzon, an Attorney General who received the order in 1705 and died in 1708. Made by Daniel Steinweg, Tønder, probably 1705—08. Height 11.8 cms.   Privately owned.

76. (See opp., top right). Gold beaker, plain. On the side, King Frederick IV's cypher, repeated and reversed, with crown, in multicoloured enamel on pounced background. Probably made by Fridrich Fabritius ca. 1720—30. Height 9.6 cms.   Rosenborg.

77. (See opp., bottom left). Beaker, plain. On the side is engraved the coat of arms of Matthias Moth, a Chief Secretary, and his wife Kirstine Aagaard (who died in 1698). Made by Mogens Thommesen Løwenhertz, Horsens, about 1695. Height 10.7 cms.   Frederiksborg.

78. (See opp., bottom right). Gold beaker, plain with moulded lid. Engraved band- and leaf-work on pounced ground along the lip and on the lid around a circular panel containing King Frederick IV's cypher, repeated and reversed with crown in multicoloured enamel. Made by Fridrich Fabritius in Copenhagen 1730. Height 10 cms.   Rosenborg.

79. Beaker, plain, gilt inside, with high domed lid; in the side of the beaker are inset twelve Danish half-kroner pieces dated 1624, while a thirteenth is placed on the finial (cf. No. 58). Engraved with names Steffen Ottsen, Anna Ottsen 1733. Made by Jacob v. Holten, Copenhagen 1733. Height 11.5 cms. Privately owned.

80. Goblet, oval, fluted, with moulded foot and moulded lid. On the side is an engraved ornament with rococo leaves. The beaker was made in Copenhagen 1702, but was completely re-made and newly ornamented by Andreas Brøndlund in Copenhagen 1750. Height 15 cms.
Privately owned.

81. Double beaker, barrel-shaped (cf. Nos. 98 and 99). Made by Axel J. Krøyer in Copenhagen 1735. Height 10.3 cms. Privately owned.

82. Beaker, curving inwards below the middle, resting on three curved feet with rococo shells. On the side a festoon of leaves is engraved around the initials of the owner, which have been pricked in at a much later date. Made by Andreas Jacob Rudolph, Copenhagen 1756. Height 10.6 cms. Privately owned.

83. Beaker with leaf ornaments engraved around three circular panels; in one is engraved the owners' initials and the date 1783, in the second a flower and in the third an anvil with tongs and hammer. Made by Johannes Zønnichsen Buxlund, Aarhus. Height 11.4 cms. Privately owned.

84. Beaker, with lid; twisted fluting; flower-shaped finial. Made by Arved Hansen, Copenhagen 1769. Height 15.7 cms. Privately owned.

85. So-called »Mill beaker«; a beaker, silver parcel-gilt, forms the base of a mill with oblique blow-pipe; by blowing through this the arms are set in motion. The point was to empty the beaker while the mill went round. Drinking-vessels of this and many other curious forms were often used in the Renaissance period; they were occasionally, as in this case, produced later. Made by Gottfred Bolch, Copenhagen 1709. Height 23.5 cms.

Danish National Museum.

86. Beaker, in the form of a tumbler (cf. No. 88 and Nos. 90—92), resting on three gadrooned ball feet. On the side are engraved the coat of arms and initials of Jørgen Brahe, a Councillor of State, and his wife Anne Helvig Thott, with the date 1705. Made by Matthis Simonsen in Odense. Height 8.5 cms. Privately owned.

Besides the ordinary tankards there appeared, both during and after the Renaissance, small beakers which were certainly used for brandy. They were often miniature editions of the big beakers, as shown in No. 87. In the Baroque period and later tumblers were often used; these were small beakers shaped almost like a hemisphere, and their function is described in a German verse which is sometimes met with on Danish tumblers and which reads in translation: »Drink me up and put me down; if I stand up, then fill me again.« A special form of beaker has the form of a flattened oval, well adapted for use when travelling, etc. (No. 89 — cf. No. 80).

87. (See opp., top left). Brandy beaker. Engraved with names: Pale Dyre — Maria Grube — 1676. Made by unknown Danish goldsmith. Height 3.7 cms. Frederiksborg.

88. (See opp., top right). Gold tumbler with King Frederick IV's cypher, repeated and reversed with crown in multicoloured enamel on pounced ground (cf. No. 76). Probably made by Fridrich Fabritius, Copenhagen, about 1720—30. Height 5.4 cms. Rosenborg.

89. (See opp., left centre). Tumbler, oval, plain, gilt inside. Made by Jens Pedersen Komløv, Copenhagen 1716. Height 6.2 cms. Cross measurements 8.7 × 5.5 cms.

Privately owned.

90. (See opp., right centre). Tumbler chased with hunting scenes and leaf-work. Made by Jørgen Stilche, Copenhagen 1686. Height 3.8 cms. Privately owned.

91. (See opp., bottom left). Tumbler, plain, with gilt rim. Made by Christen Jensen, Copenhagen 1708. Height 4.2 cms. Privately owned.

92. (See opp., bottom right). Tumbler chased with neo-classical swags and medallions. Made by Cort Legan Rasmussen in Copenhagen about 1780—90. Height 3.6 cms.

Privately owned.

Small schnapps goblets appear frequently from the middle of the 18th Century onwards. Here are four different types, all belonging to »Den gamle by« (The Old Town Museum) in Aarhus.

93. Schnapps goblet, with simple chased ornament, the initials of the owners and the date 1764 pricked in the surface. Made by Knud Brandt, Horsens. Height 12 cms.

94. Schnapps goblet with engraved border. Made by Christian Høvring, Randers (master craftsman 1767—82) or his widow (died some time after 1794). Height 11.7 cms.

95. Schnapps goblet with engraved festoons and angular stem with facetted knob. Probably made by Nielst Holst Wendelboe, Aarhus, ca. 1790—1800. Height 12.6 cms.

96. Schnapps goblet lightly engraved with ornaments in classical style and owners' name with date 1822. Made by Carl Christian Hansen, Aarhus. Height 12 cms.

97. Wine jug, pear-shaped, with foot; curved spout ending in dragon's head. Beaded curved handle. Cast thumb-piece. Engraved Renaissance ornament; roped borders around the foot. On the body and lid are engraved the crown and escutcheon of Frederick II (died 1588) with the monogram FS (Fredericus Secundus). Tankards of this type, which go back to the Middle Ages, must have been quite common in the Renaissance period, but in Denmark the only surviving example is the one shown in the illustration. Height 23.6 cms. Rosenborg.

98. Jug (»Pipe Tankard«), conical, the upper and lower sections chased with hoops. The tankard is made to imitate cooper's work (cf. Nos. 81 and 99); wooden tankards of the same form made with osier bands date from the same period. Thumbpiece in the form of a crow. On the plain band are engraved the coat of arms and initials of Lieutenant General Palle Krag and his wife Helle Trolle. On the bottom is engraved »Sanct Oluffs dags markens Gaffue Anno 1704« (»Fair of St. Olaf's Day, 1704«). Made by Johan H. Plumb, Aarhus (master craftsman 1686—1721). Height 21 cms.

Danish National Museum.

99. Jug (»Pipe Tankard«), gilt, swelling side chased with hoops around the upper and lower parts. Engraved with vertical lines in imitation of cooper's work. On the lid is cast a Norwegian lion. Made by Jens Christensen, Copenhagen 1732. Height 26 cms.

Privately owned.

100. Coffee-pot, oval, plain, on four legs with handle and knob of black wood. On the side are engraved the crown and coat of arms of Queen Anna Sophie as Duchess of Schleswig. Communion flagons of similar form to this and Nos. 102 and 103 may be found among the Church plate dating from the Baroque period. A special feature of the coffee-pot is the wooden handle and finial. Made in Copenhagen 1717, probably by Nicolai Junge. Height 22.5 cms.   Frederiksborg.

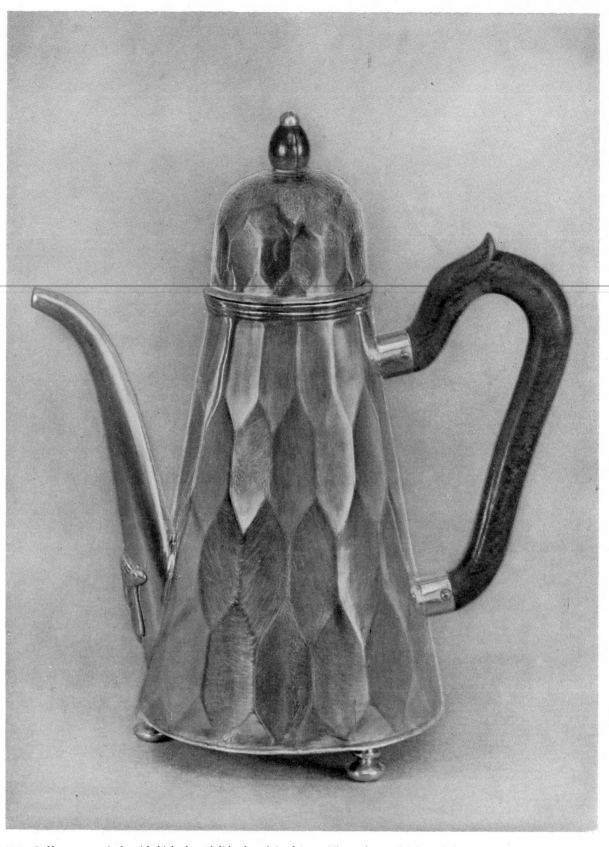

101. Coffee-pot, conical, with high domed lid, chased in facets. Three feet. Finial and handle of black wood. The coffee-pot reveals English influence and is of a type unusual in Denmark. Made by Morten Christensen Kirchhof, Copenhagen 1718. Height 20 cms.   Privately owned.

102. Coffee-pot, with swelling body, handle and finial of black wood (as regards form cf. No. 100). Engraved strapwork. Spout, with cast masks. Radial chased gadrooning around finial and rim of lid. Made by Morten Christensen Kirchhof, Copenhagen, 1719. Height 24 cms.   Frederiksborg.

103. Coffee pot, plain, pear-shaped, with moulded base and wooden handle (the lower end broken off). The finial has a washer of dark wood. On the side is engraved Queen Anna Sophie's cypher, repeated and reversed with crown. Made by Jens Christensen, Copenhagen, 1727. Height 24.5 cms.   Privately owned.

104. Coffee-pot, plain, pear-shaped, with base, curved spout, pine-cone finial, silver handle. On the side is an engraved cartouche with cyphers, repeated and reversed. Made by Peter Normand, Randers, about 1750. Height 30 cms.

Privately owned.

105. Coffee-pot, with swelling body, oval section, with base. Fluted, with chased flowers and rococo shells (cf. No. 135). Handle and fluted finial of black wood. Made by Jens Kieldsen Sommerfeldt, Aalborg, about 1760. Height 25 cms. Privately owned.

106. Coffee-pot, with swelling body, oval section, with base. Fluted and engraved with frosted flower tendrils. Handle and fluted finial of black wood. Made by Jens Kieldsen Sommerfeldt, Aalborg, about 1760. Height 27.5 cms. Privately owned.

107. Coffee-pot, with swelling body, oval section, resting on three curved legs. Fluted, with chased rococo shells. Flower-shaped finial. Black wooden handle. Made by Jens Kieldsen Sommerfeldt, Aalborg, about 1760. Height 27 cms. Privately owned.

108. Coffee-pot, with swelling body, fluted, with three legs, fluted finial and handle of black wood; the companion pieces are a tea-pot with two tea-canisters, also fluted. On the tea-canisters is pricked the owner's name with date 1749. Made for B. Simonsen of Elvedgaard by Søren Nielsen Bruun, Odense about 1749. Heights: Coffe-pot 24.8 cms, Tea-pot 11.8 cms, Tea-canisters 15 cms.   Privately owned.

109. Coffee-pot, with swelling body, oval, black wood handle, dish to match, all fluted. Most of the 18th Century coffee- or tea-pots made without legs must have had a matching dish, which in most cases has since disappeared. On the side of the pot is engraved the coat of arms of the Bertouch family. Made by Christopher Jonsen, Copenhagen 1749. Height 19.1 cms.   Privately owned.

110. Coffee-pot, with swelling body, fluted, on four curved legs. Fluted finial and handle of black wood. Made by Jens Christensen, Copenhagen, in the 1750's. Height 27.5 cms. Privately owned.

111. Coffee-pot, with swelling body, three curved shell legs. Hat-shaped lid (French type) with cast bird as finial. Small spout made in the form of a dragon's head. Handle of black wood fastened to a dragon's head. Spiral and twisted fluting with rococo shells. Made by Nicolai Langermann, Copenhagen, 1756. Height 28 cms. Privately owned.

112. Coffee-pot, with swelling body, twisted fluting. on three curved legs. Cast bird as finial. Spout shaped like a dragon's head. Black wood handle. Made by Arved Hansen, Copenhagen, 1766. Height 23.5 cms. Privately owned.

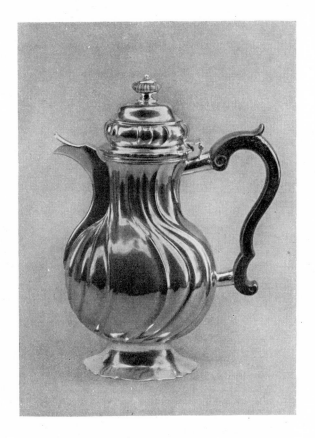

113. Coffee-pot, oval, with swelling body, twisted fluting, with base. (Shape as in No. 103, cf. No. 109). Fluted finial and handle of black wood. Made by Søren Jensen Klitgaard, Copenhagen, 1763. Height 24.4 cms.

Privately owned.

114. Coffee-pot, with swelling body, round, twisted fluting, with base. Rococo decoration on the spout. Both the handle and the washer inserted in the finial are of black wood. Owner's initials and date 1752 pricked in. Made by Knud Brandt in Horsens ca. 1752. Height 29 cms. Privately owned.

115. Coffee-pot, low, round, with swelling body, twisted fluting, resting on three cast, curved legs with flowers in relief. Curved spout with leaf festoons (a neo-classical feature) terminating in a dragon's head. Bird as finial. Handle of dark wood. On the side are engraved the initials, crown and motto of King Christian VII together with the date »26th July 1781« (the coffee-pot was given as a prize at the Royal Game Shoot held on that day). Made by Andreas Røymand, Copenhagen, 1781. Height 18.5 cms. Privately owned.

116. Coffee-pot, with swelling body, round, on three legs. Bird as finial. Neo-classical festoons of leaves carved on the body. Turned black wooden handle. Made by Johan Georg Høderich, Copenhagen, 1779. Height 20.5 cms.   Privately owned.

117. Gold coffee-pot, with swelling body, round, on three legs. Turned wooden handle, black. Rococo shells in relief on the spout. Fluting with cross-bands (fasces) on the edge of the lid and the bush of the handle. Frosted ornaments, early neo-classical style. The coffee-pot is in French rococo form and belongs to the gold service illustrated in the Introduction. Made by Thomas Westrup, Copenhagen, 1761. — Height 22 cms.   Rosenborg.

118. Chocolate pot, cylindrical, on three legs. Loose lid with drop handle; in the lid is a hole closed by a cover, which can be turned to allow for the insertion of a stick with which to stir the chocolate. Turned wooden handle, black. Made by Jørgen Friis, Randers ca. 1790. Height 18.7 cms.
                Privately owned.

119. Coffee-pot, cylindrical, with loose lid; finial a fruit with leaf. Turned wooden handle, black. Similar coffee-pots were very common in Sweden from the 1780's; probably the cylindrical type derives from there. Made by Jon Jonsen, Copenhagen, 1801. Height 18 cms. Privately owned.

120. Coffee-pot, egg-shaped, with base (cf. No. 122), and curved spout; handle of black wood. Engraved with simple stylised leaf border and medallion with King Christian VII's crown and initials and the date »11th August 1791«. (The pot was a prize awarded for the Royal Game Shoot in which the Royal Copenhagen Shooting Club took part on that date). Made by unknown Danish goldsmith ca. 1791. Height 18 cms.
Privately owned.

121. Coffee-pot, with curved sides, moulded, domed lid. Black, slightly curved wooden handle. Lightly engraved with stylised leaf-borders and festoons, with medallion containing monogram. The ornamentation is typical of the period approx. 1790—1805. As regards form cf. No. 123. Made by Bendix Gijsen, Copenhagen 1798. Height 18 cms.
Privately owned.

122. Coffee-pot, vase-shaped, curved spout with dragon's head, handle of black wood. Chased neo-classical ornaments, including festoons with oval medallions and bows. Both this vase form and the previously illustrated, more simple egg form (No. 120) are typically neo-classical. Made by Johan Henrich Kemerer, Copenhagen 1790. Height 32 cms.

Privately owned.

125. Coffee-pot, vase-shaped with loose lid; curved spout with dragon's head. Chased gadrooning and leaf borders. On the lid a lion couchant. Handle of black wood. Made by Levin Dyrkopf, Copenhagen 1830.   Privately owned.

123. (See opp., above). Coffee-pot, with curved sides, and curved spout. Loose lid surrounded by raised collar. Finial and handle of black wood. Around the upper half of the pot is a border with grapes and vine-leaves, festoons and shield cartouches in bas-relief. The form of the coffee-pot resembles that of English plated ware; the border is a special ornament of the Danish Empire style. Made by Niels Ebbesen, Copenhagen 1812. Height 17 cms.   Danish Museum of Decorative Art.

124. (See opp., below). Coffee-pot, plain, oval, with swelling sides, moulded top and raised collar surrounding a loose domed lid; curved spout. Fluted finial and handle of black wood. Made by Johan Martin Lercke, Copenhagen 1821. Height 22 cms.   Privately owned.

126. Tea-pot. Domed lid. Handle and washer in finial are of black wood. Strapwork engraved on the upper part of body and lid. Tea-pots of this form are known in England from the beginning of the 18th Century. Made by Steffen Lemmick, Aalborg, (master craftsman 1699—1745). Height 12.4 cms.   Privately owned.

127. Tea-pot; low domed lid; handle of black wood. Chased radial gadrooning and band ornaments; on the lid are chased leaves, with small radial gadrooning on the edge. Form and decoration point to the beginning of the 18th Century, but the workmanship is rather provincial. Made by Christen Olesen, Vejle, (master craftsman 1706—43). Height 10.5 cms.   Privately owned.

128. Tea-pot, fluted; domed lid; finial and handle of black wood. Made by Oluf Clausen, Odense, (master crafts-man 1706—17) or more likely, his widow (died 1738). Height 12.7 cms.   Privately owned.

129. Tea-pot, fluted; domed lid; finial and handle of black wood. Made by Jørgen Bager, Horsens, c. 1755. Height 14.5 cms.   Privately owned.

130. Tea-pot, plain, oval; moulded lid with four shallow flutings. Finial and handle of black wood. The plain tea-pot is of a type that goes back to the beginning of the 18th Century, but the fluted lid proves this example to have been of somewhat later origin. Made by Sivert Thorsteinsson, Copenhagen, 1747. Height 13.5 cms.

Privately owned.

131. Tea-pot, fluted, moulded lid; three legs with lion paws, resting on half balls. Finial and handle of black wood. It is unusual for tea-pots made before the Rococo period to have legs. Made by Anders Brasen, Randers, 1745. Height 15.5 cms.   Privately owned.

132. (See opp., above). Tea-pot, fluted; moulded lid; wooden washer in finial and carved handle of black wood. Fluted oval dish to match (cf. No. 109). Made by Hans Bruun, Sønderborg, (master craftsman 1736—59).

Privately owned.

133. (See opp., below). Tea-pot, fluted, with moulded lid; finial and handle of bone. Fluted oval dish to match (cf. No. 109 and 132). Made by Detleff Pape, Copenhagen, 1747. Height 14.5 cms.

Privately owned.

134. Tea-pot, with swelling body and three curved feet; handle of black wood. Spiral-shaped fluting (cf. No. 111) and chased rococo decoration on the side. Cast bird as finial. Made by Jacob Andersen Bechsted, Copenhagen 1760.   Privately owned.

135. Tea-pot, fluted, with engraved rococo decoration, resting on three curved feet. Curved spout cast with leaves and masks. Bird as finial. Bone handle. It is characteristic of the Aalborg goldsmiths that they continued until late into the Rococo period to use straight fluting together with chased or engraved Rococo ornaments (cf. for example No. 107). Made by Povel Knudsen Lund, Aalborg (master craftsman 1767—1794). Height 17 cms.   Privately owned.

136. Tea-pot, with twisted fluting; moulded lid with cast bird; curved spout terminating in dragon's head. Three leaf-shaped feet. Handle of light wood. Made by Søren Knie, Kalundborg ca. 1760—70. Height 15 cms.   Privately owned.

137. Tea-pot, with twisted fluting, three curved feet, washer in finial and carved handle of dark wood. Made by Berthold Sørensen Rosendahl, Aabenraa ca. 1760—70. Height 16.5 cms.

Privately owned.

138. Tea-pot, with twisted fluting, handle of dark wood; dish to match. Made by Nicolai Langermann, Copenhagen, 1757. Height 11.3 cms.   C. L. Davids Fund and Collection.

139. Gold tea-pot with three feet; low domed lid; horizontal fluting with diagonal cross-bands (fasces) along the edge of the lid; flower-shaped finial. The tea-pot is in a French Rococo form. Frosted ornaments, early neo-classical. Carved gilt wooden handle. Part of gold service illustrated in the Introduction (cf. Nos. 117 and 192). Made by Thomas Westrup, Copenhagen 1762. Height 11 cms.   Rosenborg.

140. Tea-pot, bowl-shaped, square base; lid slightly domed. Chased neo-classical (Louis XVI) ornaments. Dragon's head spout. Dragon-shaped handle of black wood. Made by Andreas Røymand,
Copenhagen 1777. Height 12.3 cms.   Privately owned.

141. Tea-pot, chased neo-classical (Louis XVI) ornaments (garlands with medallions etc.). Three legs.
Handle of dark wood. Made by Jon Jonsen, Copenhagen 1781. Height 14.1 cms.
Danish Museum of Decorative Art.

142. Tea-pot, spheroid, three curved feet. Lightly engraved ornaments, early neo-classical style. Fruit-shaped finial and handle of black wood. Made by Christian Hosøe, Copenhagen 1781. Height 12.5 cms.   Privately owned.

143. Tea-pot, oval, with slightly curved side; fluted edges. Around the bottom and on the lid are chased pointed leaves, around the top a narrow engraved border. Finial and handle of black wood. This tea-pot and the five following have English prototypes of the same period. Made by unknown Copenhagen goldsmith 1789. Height 15 cms.
»Den gamle by« (Old Town Museum), Aarhus.

144. Tea-pot, plain, spheroid, with plaited straw-handle; loose lid surrounded by raised collar. For shape, cf. No. 143. Made by Pierre Frontin, Copenhagen ca. 1800. Height 12 cms.   Danish Museum of Decorative Art.

145. Tea-pot, oval, with slightly curved side. Plain, fluted edges. Small hinged lid with flower-shaped finial. Handle of black wood. A companion piece to cream jug No. 155; for shape cf. No. 143. Made by Peter Ulrich Walerius, Copenhagen 1806. Height 15 cms.   Privately owned.

146. Tea-pot, oval, with straight sides. Lightly engraved with vine ornaments. Loose lid surrounded by a gallery. Finial and handle of black wood. For shape, cf. No. 143. Made by Christian Hosøe, Copenhagen 1807. Height 15 cms.

Danish National Museum.

147. Tea-pot, oval, slightly curved side; around the top a border chased with vine-leaves and two wide shield cartouches. Loose lid surrounded by raised collar. Cf. Nos. 123 and 143. Made by Franciscus Kozlowsky, Copenhagen 1812. Height 14.6 cms.

Privately owned.

148. Tea-pot, four-sided, with rounded ends and plain, slightly swelling side, lightly engraved with leaf and vine borders at the top and bottom. Loose domed lid surrounded by a gallery. Finial and handle of black wood. For shape, cf. No. 143. Under the bottom is pricked the date 1817. Made by Jürgen Joachim Jürgensen, Sønderborg, ca. 1817. Height 13 cms.   Privately owned.

149. Tea-pot, low, curved sides with vertical gadrooning; small loose lid surrounded by raised collar. Spout shaped like an animal. Finial and handle of black wood. Made by A. Michelsen, Copenhagen 1843 after drawing by G. F. Hetsch (probably inspired by Roman lamp). Height 10.5 cms (with handle 14 cms).   Privately owned.

150. Tea-kettle, with swelling sides and twisted fluting; wide chased gadrooning and engraved leaf border around upper rim; high domed lid with twisted fluting and gadrooned edge. Spout with animal's head, movable handle with turned black wooden hand grip. Loose tripod, not originally belonging to the kettle, with a spirit lamp of more recent date. The kettle was made by Thomas Westrup, Copenhagen 1786, the tripod by an unknown Copenhagen master craftsman in 1733 and the spirit lamp by H. H. Schmidt, Copenhagen ca. 1800. Height (with tripod and handle raised) 34 cms.   Privately owned.

151. Tea-kettle, resting on loose tripod with black turned knobs and spirit-lamp. The kettle is oval, plain, and with rounded sides. Loose lid with wooden finial. Movable bow-handle. Made by Friedrich Wissing, Odense (master craftsman 1745—70). Height (with tripod and handle raised) 29.5 cms.   Privately owned.

152. Tea-kettle, with swelling sides and twisted fluting; low domed lid with cast bird. Movable bow handle with turned black wooden hand grip. Loose tripod with spirit lamp. On the kettle the letters S L are engraved below a seven-pointed coronet (probably signifying Baron Severin Løvenskiold). Made by Christopher Jonsen, Copenhagen 1772. Height (with tripod and handle raised) 34.5 cms.
                    Privately owned.

153. Coffee percolator, cylindrical, with smaller detachable top. Plain, fluted edges and engraved coat-of-arms, representing the Rosencrantz and Raben families. Fluted finial and handle of black wood. Stand with spirit lamp. Made by C. C. F. Schrøder, Copenhagen 1835. Height 33 cms.   Privately owned.

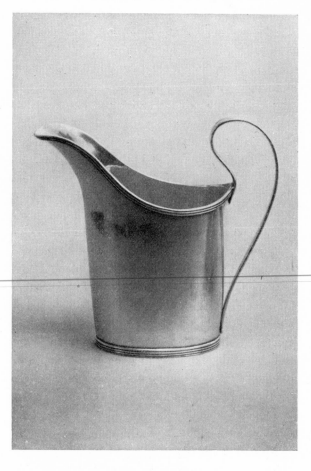

154. Cream jug, oval, fluted. Under the base are pricked the owner's initials and the date 1748. Made by Knud Brandt, Horsens ca. 1748. Height 8.9 cms.

»Den gamle by« (The Old Town Museum), Aarhus.

155. Cream jug, plain, oval, fluted edges, gilt inside. Companion piece to tea-pot, No. 145. Made by Peter Ulrich Walerius, Copenhagen 1806. Height 12 cms.

Privately owned.

156. Cream jug, with four slightly curved sides, plain, with fluted rims; border chased with vine leaves and broad shield cartouches (cf. No. 123). Made by Abraham Nyemann, Copenhagen 1813. Height 15.7 cms.

Privately owned.

157. Tea-urn, bulbous, fluted, four curved legs and movable handles with mussel-shaped lugs. The bottom is grated to allow a draught for charcoal firing, and at the top is a smoke outlet. Made by Nicolai Junge, Copenhagen 1739. Height 39.5 cms.   Privately owned.

158. Tea urn, bulbous, plain resting on three curved legs with lion feet, made at a later date. Two detachable bow handles of black wood. On the front is engraved the crown and cypher, repeated and reversed, of Queen Anna Sophie. Grated bottom and smoke escape as in No. 157. Made by Asmus Fridrich Holling, Copenhagen 1739; legs re-made by P. Kragh, Copenhagen ca. 1800. Height 41.5 cms.

Privately owned.

159. Tea-urn, bulbous, with twisted fluting. Two fixed handles. Grated bottom and smoke outlet (cf. No. 157). Engraved with coat-of-arms of Count Schack Brockdorff (died 1761) and his wife Sophie Hedevig Grabow. Made by Knud Brandt, Horsens ca. 1760. Height 48 cms.   Privately owned.

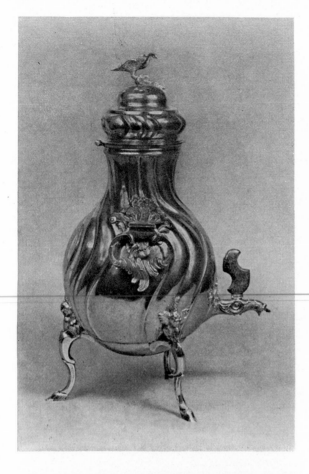

160. Tea urn (holding warm water; without firing), bulbous, twisted fluting, movable handles with rococo shells; three curved legs. High moulded hinged lid decorated with twisted fluting and surmounted by a bird. Made by Johan Henrik Røschke, Copenhagen 1762. Height 34 cms. Privately owned.

161. Tea urn (without firing), bulbous, chased with c-shaped gadrooning (cf. No. 134) and flower-stalks; projecting handles cast with mussels; three curved legs. On the high domed, chased lid is a cast bird. Made by Johan Jacob Schrader, Copenhagen 1769. Height 35.5 cms. Privately owned.

162. Tea urn (without firing), slender, bulbous, with twisted fluting; on the lid is an eagle. Three curved shell legs. Two projecting wood-lined handles. Made by Hans Busch, Aalborg ca. 1775. Height 34.5 cms. Privately owned.

163. Tea urn (without firing), bulbous, with twisted fluting, chased rococo shells along the flutings. Drop handles. Three curved legs with shell feet. On the lid is cast a sea-monster. Made by Sivert Thorsteinsson, Copenhagen 1753. Height 34 cms.

Privately owned.

164. Tea urn, bulbous, with twisted fluting, chased rococo decoration and flowers. Three cast legs adorned with scrolls; drop handles. Grated bottom and smoke escape as in No. 157. Made by unknown Copenhagen goldsmith in the 1760's. Height 47.5 cms.   Danish Museum of Decorative Art.

165. Tea urn, bulbous, plain, with drop handles, the lugs embellished with shells, three curved legs with spirit-lamp. Engraved early neo-classical ornaments and coat-of-arms with the insignia of the most distinguished order of Dannebrog showing that the urn once belonged to Baron Iver Rosencrantz and his wife Marie Elisabeth Lente Adeler. Made by Christopher Jonsen, Copenhagen 1768. Height 46.5 cms.

Privately owned.

166. Tea urn, neo-classical urn shape with square plinth on four lion feet. Chased gadrooning, leaf garlands and festoons with medallions. Drop handles, each a leaf garland set in a lion mask. Grated bottom and smoke escape as in No. 157. Made by Thomas Westrup, Copenhagen 1776. Height 47 cms.   Privately owned.

167. Tea urn (without firing), vase-shaped, with chased neo-classical (Louis XVI) ornaments. Two handles in the form of mermaids. Engraved crown and cypher F repeated and reversed (representing Crown Prince Frederik (VI) or Frederik the heir presumptive). Made by Christian Werum, Copenhagen 1788. Height 34.5 cms.   Privately owned.

168. Tea urn, vase-shaped; chased gadrooning, leaves and festoons of drapery with medallions adorned with flowers. Drop ring handles. Made by Christian Werum, Copenhagen 1790.   Privately owned.

169. Tea urn and two tea canisters, egg-shaped with engraved festoons, high fluted handles. On the base of the urn is engraved in Danish: »Given by H. R. H. the Crown Prince 30th Nov. 1790«. Made by Christian N. Hosøe, Copenhagen 1790. Heights: Tea urn 35.2 cms. Tea canisters 15 cms.   Privately owned.

170. Tea urn (without firing), vase-shaped, lightly engraved with vines, tall curved handles. Made by Andreas Holm, Copenhagen 1798. Height 34 cms.

Danish National Museum.

171. Tea urn, spherical, plain; four curved legs with lion paws. Plinth on four ball feet. Ring handles set in lion masks. In the middle of the plinth is a spherical spirit lamp. A companion piece to tea-pot No. 145 and jug No. 155. Made by Peter Ulrich Walerius, Copenhagen 1806. Height 34 cms. Privately owned.

172. Tea urn, round, with chased gadrooning, handles in form of goat's horn with wooden grip and four curved legs on square plinth with lion paws. Original spirit lamp has been renewed. Made by Copenhagen goldsmith (probably Hans Jacob Møller), 1832. Height 33 cms.

Privately owned.

173. Tea urn, four-sided container with frieze of acanthus leaf-work, laurel sprays and dragons surrounding two shields in bas-relief. High, stepped lid with cylindrical, perpendicular, openwork chimney. Grated bottom, as in No. 157. Ring handles set in lion masks. Four fluted legs slightly curved with lion paws resting on plinth on four ball feet. Made by Abraham Nyemann, Copenhagen 1811. Height 53 cms.

Danish National Museum.

174. (See opp., above). Tea canister, with two compartments for different sorts of tea; rectangular shape, plain, with moulded edges. Two sliding lids with knobs. Engraved with the initials of the owners (commoners) and »Anno 1701«. Made by Didrich Hoff, Copenhagen 1701. Height 7.7 cms.   Privately owned.

175. (See opp., below). Tea canister, with two compartments, plain, with moulded edges. Sliding lid at the top and bottom. Roundel containing flowers engraved around the owner's initials and »Anno 1706«. Made by Didrich Hoff, Copenhagen 1701. Height 10.4 cms.
                              Privately owned.

176. Tea canister with domed cap. On each side a bunch of fruit is chased in a square pounced panel. Made by Nicolaus Fuchs, Copenhagen 1708. Height 11.5 cms.
                              Privately owned.

177. Tea canister with domed cap. Engraved strapwork on pounced ground. Made by Christen Jensen, Copenhagen 1729. Height 13.7 cms.
                              Privately owned.

178. Tea canister, hexagonal, plain, with domed cap. Engraved with initials of the owners (commoners) and the date 1737. Made by Jens Pedersen Komløv, Copenhagen 1737. Height 15.5 cms.   Privately owned.

179. Tea canister, octagonal, plain, with moulded base and domed cap. Garland of leaves engraved around the owners' initials and the date 1742. Made by Sivert Thorsteinsson, Copenhagen 1742. Height 13 cms.   Privately owned.

180. Tea canister, oblong, with fluted corners, moulded base and upper edge, sliding lid with knob. Made by Ole Flores Wilcken, Copenhagen 1733. Height 8.5 cms. Frederiksborg.

181. Tea canister, oblong, plain, with moulded upper edge, sliding lid with knob. Made by Lorentz Nielsen, Copenhagen 1729. Height 8.4 cms.   Privately owned.

182. Tea canister, oval, with vertical fluting; domed cap. Made by Knud Brandt, Horsens ca. 1740—50. Height 11.8 cms.   Privately owned.

183. Tea canister, cylindrical, plain, with two compartments; at each end is a loose lid with moulded edges. In the lids are engraved the letters B and G respectively, probably indicating Bohe tea and green tea. Made by Peter Norman, Randers ca. 1750. Height 7.8 cms.

     Privately owned.

184. Tea canister, bulbous, oval, resting on three leaf-shaped feet. Loose domed lid with cast bird. Fluted, with chased rococo shells (cf. No. 135). Made by Hans Budtz Sommerfeldt, Aalborg ca. 1760—70. Height 13 cms.

Privately owned.

185. Tea canister, round, bulbous, with twisted fluting; three leaf-shaped feet and domed cap with cast bird. Made by Børge Lemmich, Copenhagen 1757. Height 13 cms.　　　　　　　　　　　Privately owned.

186. Tea canister, conical, with domed cap. Sides chased with three series of flutings, convex and concave alternating. Made by Jens Isachsen Friis, Ringkøbing (master craftsman 1724—55). Height 11.6 cms.

Historical Museum, Aalborg.

187. Tea canister, round, bulbous, with base; detachable top and domed cap, on which is a cast bird. Twisted fluting. Made by Børge Mikkelsen, Aalborg ca. 1740. Height 10.7 cms.   Privately owned.

188. Tea canister, bulbous, with twisted fluting; three rococo shell feet; domed cap with cast bird. Made by Hans Busch, Aalborg ca. 1770.   Privately owned.

189. Tea canister, round, chased with strapwork. Base and lid with radial gadrooning. Made by Philip E. Jansen, Sønderborg ca. 1760. Height 14 cms.

                    Privately owned.

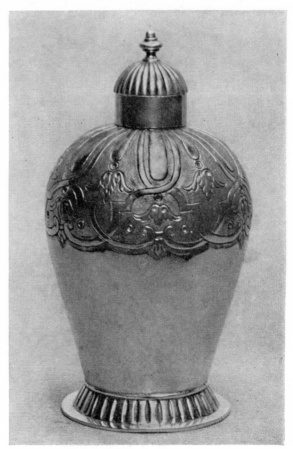

190. Tea canister, with swelling sides, detachable cover, domed cap, cast and engraved garlands of leaves with cross-bands around the body, neck and on the cover. Engraved with Royal Danish coat-of-arms. Made by Christian Werum, Copenhagen 1778. Height 16 cms.

Royal Household Silver.

191. Tea canister, egg-shaped, with domed cap. Plain; the lid, top and base with beaded edge. Engraved with Royal Danish coat-of-arms. Made by Christian Hosøe, Copenhagen 1790. Height 12.8 cms. Royal Household Silver.

192. Gold tea canister, plain, with swelling sides, detachable top and domed cap. Frosted symmetrical ornaments of early neo-classical design. Around the base and top are horizontal flutings with bands (fasces). Belongs to the gold service illustrated in the Introduction (cf. Nos. 117 and 139). Made by Thomas A. Westrup, Copenhagen 1762. Height 12.3 cms.

Rosenborg.

193. Tea canister, oval, with straight sides and domed cap; lightly engraved with leaf borders. Made by Bendix Gijsen, Copenhagen 1806. Height 8.7 cms.   Privately owned.

194. Tea canister, 16-sided, plain, with two compartments; divided in the middle. Made by Carl Frederik Dietzel, Copenhagen ca. 1815. Height 8.4 cms.   Privately owned.

195. Tea canister, oval, barrel-shaped; lower part gadrooned. Loose lid surrounded by raised collar and fine beaded edge. This and the three canisters illustrated on the next page show English influence. Made by Nicolai Christensen, Copenhagen 1817. Height 9.3 cms.   Privately owned.

196. Tea canister, cylindrical, with domed cap. Lightly engraved ornaments and owner's initials with date 1800. Made by Poul Hansen, Tønder ca. 1800. Height 10 cms.
Danish National Museum.

197. Tea canister, four-sided, sides slightly spreading, moulded lid with wooden finial. Fluted edges; border with vine leaves and shield cartouches in flat relief. The form is English; as regards ornaments, cf. No. 123. Made by Abraham Nyemann, Copenhagen 1813.

Privately owned.

198. Tea canister, barrel-shaped, with fluted edges and lightly engraved borders. Loose, slightly domed lid with fluted wooden finial, surrounded by raised latticework. Engraved with owner's initials and date 1816. Made by Erik Stridbeck, Copenhagen ca. 1816.

Privately owned.

199. Tea canister, oval, with straight sides, slightly domed lid with black wooden finial. Beaded edges. Engraved borders and festoon of drapery with medallion dated 1797. Made by Johan Fridrich Ekstrøm, Copenhagen 1797. Height 11 cms.

Danish National Museum.

200. Mahogany case with silver mountings, containing two plain oblong tea canisters with loose caps and a sugar container, oblong, with curved, hinged lid; on the lid is engraved a coat-of-arms (Rosencrantz impaling another). Made by Frederik Janus Creutzberg, Aarhus (master craftsman 1784—1826). Height of tea canisters 8.7 cms. Height of sugar box 9.8 cms.   Privately owned.

201. (See opp., above). Silver box, with hinged lid, probably for sugar. Oblong, plain, gilt inside. Moulded edges, four ball feet. On the side is engraved an unknown coat-of-arms with initials JL and BD; on the lid a cypher THP repeated and reversed. Made by Didrich Hoff, Copenhagen, 1701. Height 9 cms.   Privately owned.

202. (See opp., below). Sugar box, oval and fluted with loose moulded cover. Engraved with crown and monogram of Queen Sophie Magdalene. Part of that queen's tea- and coffee-service, which is preserved among the Royal Household Silver. Made by Tyge Madsen Werum, Copenhagen, 1740. Height 6.9 cms.
    The Royal Household Silver

203. Silver box with moulded hinged lid, oval, with twisted fluting. Probably for sugar; vessels of corresponding form are used also for toilet powder etc. Made by Christopher Jonsen, Copenhagen 1752. Height 11.7 cms.
    Privately owned.

204. Gold sugar box, round, with swelling sides, resting on three feet; low, domed, loose lid with flower bud as finial. Frosted ornaments, early neo-classical; the lid has a fluted edge with diagonal cross-bands (fasces). Part of the gold service illustrated in the Introduction (cf. Nos. 117, 139 and 192). Made by Thomas Westrup, Copenhagen 1762. Height 9 cms.   Rosenborg.

205. Sugar-dredger, cylindrical, domed lid with engraved and pierced leaf-decoration. Gilt edges. On the side is a round gilt panel engraved with the coat-of-arms and initials of the owner, a commoner, with the date 1677. This oldest type of Danish sugar-dredger has English prototypes of the same period. Made by Peter Rasmussen, Viborg ca. 1677. Height 19.5 cms.
Privately owned.

206. Sugar-dredger of same form. On the side are engraved the coats-of-arms and initials of Otte Bielke and his wife Beate Rosencrantz, with the date 1700. Made by Claus Lauritzen Lave, Copenhagen, ca. 1700.
Privately owned.

207. Sugar-dredger of the same form. On the side are engraved the coats-of-arms of the families Arenfeldt and Mühlheim. Made by Gottfred Bolch, Copenhagen 1707, probably for Lt. Colonel Axel Arenfeldt (died 1745) and his wife Anna Stygge Mühlheim. Height 19.5 cms.
Privately owned.

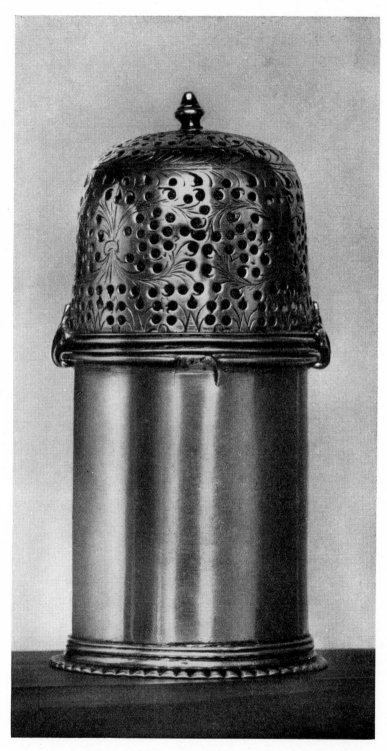

208. Sugar-dredger, cylindrical, with pierced, domed lid. Made by Simon Mathiesen, Odense, 1689. Cf. No. 205. Height 15.5 cms.   Privately owned.

209. Sugar-dredger, baluster-shaped, plain. Lid with pierced leaf decoration. Made by Jens Pedersen Komløv, Copenhagen, 1719. Height 19.7 cms.　Privately owned.

210. Sugar-dredger, baluster-shaped, plain. On the side is engraved a cypher, repeated and reversed. Made by Oluf Clausen or his widow, Odense ca. 1710—30. Height 19.2 cms.　Privately owned.

211. Sugar-dredger, baluster-shaped, plain. Lid with pierced leaf decoration. Made by Jens Pedersen Komløv, Copenhagen, 1728. Height 19.2 cms.
Danish Museum of Decorative Art.

212. Sugar-dredger; cast and fluted decoration, with shells; engraved with crown and Royal Danish coat-of-arms. Made by Jørgen Lind, Copenhagen, 1742. Height 22 cms. The Royal Household Silver.

213. Sugar-dredger, baluster-shaped, plain; pierced lid, covered by loose, plain hood. Made by Daniel Madsen Werum, Copenhagen, 1725. Height 22.3 cms. The Royal Household Silver.

214. Sugar-dredger, bulbous, fluted. Made by Christopher Jonsen, Copenhagen 1750. Height 18.1 cms.

Privately owned.

215. Sugar-dredger, bulbous, fluted. Three leaf feet. Made by Jørgen Friis, Randers ca. 1775.

Privately owned.

216. Sugar-dredger, baluster-shaped, fluted. Made by Jens Christensen, Copenhagen 1723. Height 19.3 cms.

Privately owned.

217. Sugar-dredger, bulbous, fluted. On the lid are eight panels with alternating geometrical and plant ornaments in engraved and pierced work. Made by Oluf O. Rye, Svendborg, ca. 1750. Height 20.7 cms.   Privately owned.

218. Sugar-dredger, baluster-shaped, fluted. Made by Mathias Winge, Vejle, ca. 1770. Height 19.2 cms.   Privately owned.

219. Sugar-dredger, bulbous, with twisted fluting. Made by Christopher Jonsen, Copenhagen, 1755. Height 21 cms. Privately owned.

220. Sugar-dredger, baluster-shaped, fluted. Lid with pierced leaf decoration. Made by Johannes Isachsen Lindschov, Holstebro, ca. 1740. Height 16.8 cms.
          Privately owned.

221. Sugar-dredger, pepper-pot, mustard-, oil- and vinegar-jugs with salver to match, round on spreading foot (cf. No. 395); all with twisted fluting. Made by Mathias Mortensen Bøegh, Aarhus, ca. 1770. Height of sugar-dredger 22.5 cms, other vessels 15.5 cms, tray 11.2 cms.   Privately owned.

222. Cruet. Sexfoil base on lion feet. Frame containing sugar-dredger, pepper caster, mustard pot and two salt cellars, all with twisted fluting, and two glass cruets with silver caps for oil and vinegar; brackets supporting loose openwork bowl, with twisted fluting. Under the base-plate is pricked »Plat de Menage (i. e. cruet) with brackets and basket. Øllegaard Chr. Nissen, Jac. Ch. Wassard. 1780« (Danish text translated) and the names of the various owners up to 1941 are engraved later. Made by Christian Høvring, Randers, ca. 1780; mustard pot and spoon renewed later by I. P. Struntze, Copenhagen (master craftsman 1814—54). Overall height 33 cms.   Privately owned.

223. Sugar-dredger, bulbous, with twisted fluting. Three floriated feet. Pierced leaf ornament on the lid, which is surmounted by a moulded bird with outspread wings, a prevalent motif in the second half of the 18th Century especially favoured by the goldsmiths of Aalborg. Made by Hans Budtz Sommerfeldt, Aalborg, ca. 1770. Height 19 cms.   Privately owned.

224. Sugar-dredger, bulbous; twisted fluting with chased rococo shells. On the lid is pierced leaf ornament. Three shell-shaped legs. Made by Hans Budtz Sommerfeldt, Aalborg, ca. 1770. Height 20.5 cms.   Privately owned.

225. Sugar-dredger, bulbous, curved fluting, chased rococo shells and flowers. Made by Jens Sander Schouw, Copenhagen, ca. 1775. Height 19.8 cms.   Privately owned.

226. Sugar-dredger, vase-shaped, chased with festoons of flowers, medallions and leaf borders entwined with a band. Square plinth. Companion piece to mustard pot, No. 235. Made by Hans Andreas Toldberg, Copenhagen, 1788. Height 18.3 cms.   Frederiksborg.

227. Sugar-dredger, urn-shaped, chased with neo-classical (Louis XVI) leaf festoons and medallions. Horizontal lines engraved on the plain surface. Vertical gadrooning on the lower body, base and dome of the lid. Vines are engraved and pierced in the lid. Made by Povl Knudsen Lund, Aalborg, ca. 1790. Height 20.8 cms.
                     Aalborg Museum, Aalborg.

228. Sugar-dredger, baluster-shaped, chased with neo-classical festoons of flowers. Lozengy lid pierced with crosses. Made by Niels Pihl, Copenhagen, 1776. Height 18.4 cms.   Privately owned.

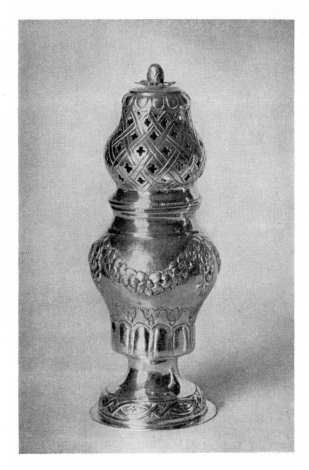

229. Pepper-pot and three containers for oil, vinegar (Danish: eddike) and mustard (Danish: sennep). Plain, bulbous, with base. Cast letters indicating the contents are employed as finials. Made by Jens Andersen, Odense (master craftsman 1703—44). Height of pepper-pot 11.6 cms, height of containers 10.8 cms.   Danish Museum of Decorative Art.

230. Cruet, the base, lower body and hinged lid gadrooned. Flat, cast thumb-piece. Scroll handle with bead moulding One of a pair of vessels, presumably for oil and vinegar. Made by Mikkel Jensen, Aalborg, at the beginning of the 18th Century. Height 9.5 cms.

Danish Museum of Decorative Art.

231. Vinegar cruet, pepper-caster and mustard-pot, bulbous, with twisted fluting, resting on three legs; on the lid a cast bird. Made by Joachim Weller, Holstebro (master craftsman ca. 1754—92). Height of pepper-caster 12 cms, height of other vessels 11 cms.

Privately owned.

232. Mustard-pot, barrel-shaped, resting on four legs. Loose lid with flower-shaped finial. Curved spoon. Made by Cort Legan Rasmussen, Copenhagen, 1778. Height 8.8 cms.　　Privately owned.

233. Pepper-caster, neo-classical urn shape with square plinth, gadrooning and leaf decoration. Made by Thomas Westrup, Copenhagen, ca. 1780. Height 12.3 cms.

Privately owned.

234. Mustard-pot, with swelling side, base and high domed lid. Chased with neo-classical festoons and leaf decoration. Made by Christian Hosøe, Copenhagen, 1788. Height 15.2 cms. Privately owned.

235. Mustard-pot, vase-shaped, chased with festoons of flowers, medallions and leaf border with entwined band. Square plinth. Made by Hans Andreas Toldberg, Copenhagen, 1788 (cf. No. 226). Height 16 cms. Spoon made at about the same time by Tyge L. Iversen, Copenhagen.

Frederiksborg.

236. Pepper-caster, baluster-shaped, plain (late Baroque design). Made by Niels Peder Høvring, Randers, ca. 1780—90. Height 12.0 cms.   Privately owned.

237. Pepper-caster, baluster-shaped, resting on square plinth. On the lid is an engraved chequered pattern and cast flower-shaped finial. Neo-classical (Louis XVI) type — cf. No. 228. Made by Nicolai Brandt, Horsens, ca. 1790. Height 13.2 cms.   Privately owned.

238. Pepper-caster, vase-shaped, on square plinth. Lightly engraved leaf ornament. Made by Nicolai Brandt, Horsens, ca. 1800. Height 13.4 cms.   Privately owned.

239. Pepper-caster, on square plinth; lightly engraved leaf and flower ornaments. Made by Fridrich Christian West, Svendborg (master craftsman 1812—34). Height 10.0 cms.
                    Privately owned.

240. Mustard-pot, vase-shaped; domed lid and bow handle. Engraved and openwork ornament. Original glass liner is missing. Spoon to match. Made by Claus Brun Alberts, Copenhagen, 1805. Height 14.2 cms.   Privately owned.

241. Salt-cellar, oval; openwork with beaded edge; four feet; blue glass liner. Made by Carl Wentzel, Copenhagen (master craftsman 1813—45). Height 4.7 cms.
Privately owned.

242. Mustard-pot, cylindrical, openwork, with peaked hinged lid, bow handle and four legs. Bead moulding and lightly engraved ornament. Blue glass liner. Made by Andreas Holm, Copenhagen, ca. 1800—10. Height 12.0 cms.
Privately owned.

243. Pepper-caster, egg-shaped; the lower part made in wire work. Blue glass liner. Made by Bendix Johan Schnee, Copenhagen, ca. 1810—1820. Height 12.0 cms.
Privately owned.

244. Mustard-pot, egg-shaped with movable bow-handle; three curved legs resting on round base. Lightly engraved ornament and owner's initials with date 1805. Made by Otto Ottosen, Vejle, ca. 1805. Height (without handle) 10.0 cms.
Privately owned.

245. Pepper-caster, vase-shaped, with egg-and-tongue border and flower ornaments. Made by C. A. T. Piil, Copenhagen, 1843. Height 10.5 cms. Privately owned.

246. Mustard-pot, vase-shaped, with hinged lid and bow handle; stamped leaf border. Made by Johan Isbrand, Copenhagen, 1828. Height 12.0 cms.
Danish Museum of Decorative Art.

247. Salt-cellar, oval, with oblique gadrooning. The inside of the bowl is gilt. Made by Thore Sørensen, Aalborg (master craftsman 1704—32). Height 4.0 cms.   Privately owned.

248. Salt-cellar, octagonal, with moulded edges. The inside of the bowl is gilt. Made by Jens Pedersen Komløv, Copenhagen, 1733. Height 4.5 cms.   Privately owned.

249. Salt-cellar, oval, fluted, with four scrolled feet. Coronet engraved over a monogram K (Knuth) repeated and reversed. Made by Jørgen N. Lind, Copenhagen, 1742. Height 3.9 cms.
Frederiksborg.

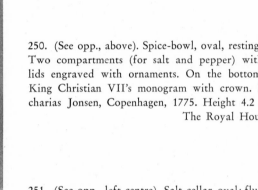

250. (See opp., above). Spice-bowl, oval, resting on four feet. Two compartments (for salt and pepper) with flat hinged lids engraved with ornaments. On the bottom is engraved King Christian VII's monogram with crown. Made by Zacharias Jonsen, Copenhagen, 1775. Height 4.2 cms.
The Royal Household Silver.

251. (See opp., left centre). Salt-cellar, oval; fluted work. The inside of the bowl is gilt. Made by Gerhard Hass, Copenhagen, 1745—49. Height 5.4 cms.   Privately owned.

252. (See opp., right centre). Salt-cellar, oval; fluted work, with chased rococo decoration. Made by Thomas A. Westrup, Copenhagen, 1769. Height 5.0 cms.   Privately owned.

253. (See opp., bottom left). Salt-cellar, oval, fluted. The inside of the bowl is gilt. Made by Jens Nielsen Randers, Copenhagen, 1747. Height 5.3 cms.   Privately owned.

254. (See opp., bottom right). Salt-cellar, oval, with twisted fluting. The bowl is gilt inside. Made by Nicolai Linde, Copenhagen, 1761. Height 5.3 cms.   Privately owned.

261. Cruet. Oval base with four feet. Filigree frame, raised handle with filigree holder for mustard-pot, surrounded by silver wire holders with three casters and two jugs, all in glass with silver lids. Made by Frederik Moritz Klose, Copenhagen 1812. Overall height 30.0 cms.   Privately owned.

255. (See opp., top left). Salt-cellar, oval, three scroll feet. Made by Søren Jensen Klitgaard, Copenhagen, 1762. Height 3.6 cms.   Frederiksborg.

256. (See opp., top right). Salt-cellar, chased with festoons and medallions, bead moulding and three legs. The inside is gilt. Made by Jens Jensen Viol, Copenhagen (master craftsman 1783—99). Height 5.5 cms.   Privately owned.

257. (See opp., left centre). Salt-cellar, boat-shaped; wire-work, oval base. Movable bow handle. Blue glass liner. Made by Meyer Nathan Levy, Copenhagen, ca. 1810—20. Height 10.0 cms.   Danish Museum of Decorative Art.

258. (See opp., right centre). Salt-cellar, round, wire-work, resting on tripod. White glass liner. Made by J. A. Boedewadt, Tønder (master craftsman 1806—44). Height 7.2 cms.   Danish Museum of Decorative Art.

259. (See opp., bottom left). Salt-cellar, boat-shaped, with oval base; two high curved bow-handles. Chased leaf border with oblong shield. Made by Johan Paul Struntze, Copenhagen, 1815. Height 8.5 cms.
Danish Museum of Decorative Art.

260. (See opp., bottom right). Salt-cellar, boat-shaped, with four feet. Chased border with leaves, flowers and oblong shield. Blue glass liner. Made by Christian Lindahl Christensen, Copenhagen, 1812. Height 6.1 cms.
Privately owned.
(Cf. salt-cellar, No. 240).

262. Spice dish with three bowl-shaped depressions. Chased flowers and leaves. In the middle is engraved a crowned monogram A R W. This little dish is of a type otherwise unknown in Denmark and its use has not so far been ascertained, but it was probably designed for the service of spice. Made by Simon Mathiesen, Odense (master craftsman 1651—97). Diameter 13.5 cms.   Privately owned.

263. Bowl (probably slop-basin), round, plain, with moulded foot. Under the fluted rim is engraved the owner's name and date: »ANNA KIRSTINE MAURETZ DAATER AAR 1703«. Made by Christian Snedker, Copenhagen, 1701. Height 10.2 cms.

Privately owned.

264. Bowl (probably slop-basin), round, chased strapwork border on matted ground. Made by Morten Christensen Kirchhof, Copenhagen, 1719. Height 7.8 cms.   Privately owned.

265. Bowl (probably slop-basin), round, fluted, on low foot. Made by Christen Jensen, Copenhagen, 1725. Height 8.5 cms.   Privately owned.

266. Bowl (identical with a slop-basin mentioned in a legacy of 1775), round, fluted, on low foot. Made by Oluf Clausen, Odense (master craftsman 1706—17), or more probably by his widow (died 1738). Height 8.0 cms.

Privately owned.

267. Bowl (probably slop-basin), round, plain, with lipped edge. Under the foot are pricked the owner's initials and the date 1734. Made by Palle Pedersen Schandorph, Aarhus, ca. 1734. Height 7.5 cms. Privately owned.

268. Bowl (probably slop-basin) oval, fluted, on low fluted foot. The inside is gilt. On the side are engraved the owner's initials and the date 1737. Made by Tyge Madsen Werum, Copenhagen, 1733. Height 6.2 cms.

Privately owned.

269. Bowl (probably slop-basin), oval, fluted, on low foot. Made by Sivert Thorsteinsson, Copenhagen, 1745. — Height 10.3 cms.   Privately owned.

270. Bowl (probably slop-basin), oval, with curved fluted sides and low, plain foot. Made by Paul Bay, Copenhagen, in the 1740's. Height 8.2 cms.
                    Privately owned.

271. Bowl, low, oval, with raised rim, fluted. Made by Philip Lorenz Weghorst, Copenhagen, 1732. Height 7.0 cms.   Privately owned.

272. Bowl (for sugar?; one of a pair), oval, with four cast leaf-shaped legs. The rim of the bowl, which curves outwards, is chased with c-shaped gadrooning and flowers. Engraved with owner's coat-of-arms. Made by Sivert Thorsteinsson, Copenhagen, ca. 1755—60. Height 6.3 cms. Privately owned.

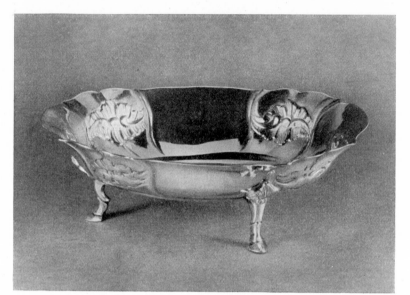

273. Bowl (for sugar or sweets?), low, oval, with twisted fluting and chased rococo ornament; three cast legs. Made by Johan Henrik Røschke, Copenhagen, 1758. Height 5.1 cms.
Privately owned.

274. Bowl (for sugar or slops?), round, with swelling side and twisted fluting. Wide collar tapering outwards. Three cast legs and two cast handles with rococo ornament. Made by Joachim Weller, Holstebro, (master craftsman 1754—92). Height 8.0 cms.
Privately owned.

275. Bowl (for sugar or sweets?), low, oval; twisted fluting. Three cast, floriated legs. Made by Bernt Christopher Kelberlade, Copenhagen 1768. Height 4.6 cms.   Privately owned.

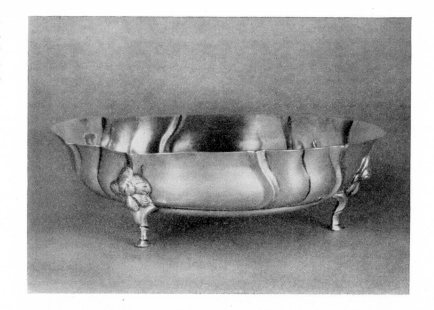

276. Bowl (for sugar?), with swelling side, scalloped edge and chased flowers. Two cast handles with rococo decoration and four cast legs. Made by Christian Werum, Copenhagen, 1772. — Height 8.2 cms.   Privately owned.

277. Bowl (for sugar or sweets), low, oval, fluted, with chased rococo decoration. Three high cast legs. Made by Christian Høvring, Randers, in 1770. Height 5.8 cms.   Privately owned.

278. Bowl (for sugar), oval, with swelling side, twisted fluting and wavy rim; three legs cast with shells. Made by Hans Busch, Aalborg, ca. 1770—80. Privately owned.

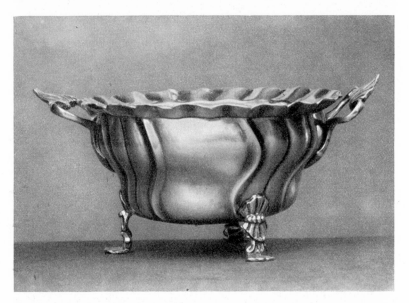

279. Bowl (for slops), a companion piece to the previous example and of about the same form, but with two cast handles with rococo decoration. Made by Hans Besch, Aalborg, 1770—80. Privately owned.

280. Bowl (for sugar?), round, with swelling side, twisted fluting, two cast handles and three cast legs. Made by Brandt Jonsen, Copenhagen, 1773. Height 7.5 cms. Privately owned.

281. Gold slop-bowl, round, with three feet. Frosted ornaments, early neo-classical style. Belongs to the gold service illustrated in the Introduction (cf. Nos. 117, 139 and 192). Made by Thomas Andreas Westrup, Copenhagen, 1761 or 1762. Height 8.4 cms.

Rosenborg.

282. Bowl (for sugar or slops?), oval, with swelling side, chased with medallions and festoons of flowers. Scalloped edge. Around the bottom is engraved a band of matted arches. Two cast handles with rococo ornament and three floriated legs. Made by Zacharias Jonsen, Copenhagen, probably in the 1780's. Height 8.0 cms.   Privately owned.

283. Bowl (for sugar or slops?), round, with swelling side; chased medallions and festoon of leaves with entwined band; wavy rim. Two cast handles decorated with rococo ornament and four legs. Made by Johan Georg Høderich, Copenhagen, 1776. Height 8.3 cms.

Privately owned.

284. Bowl (for sugar or slops?), round, with three curved legs; chased medallions and festoons of leaves. Made by Henrik Nicolai Lundsgaard, Nibe, ca. 1780. Height 8.7 cms. Privately owned.

285. Bowl, for sugar or sweets, round, with loose lid and dish. On the bowl is chased a border of leaf tendrils; the dish, lid and foot of the bowl are decorated with chased, pointed leaves; on the foot and lid are bead edgings, and on the lid is a cast rose with leaves. Made by Thomas Andreas Westrup, Copenhagen, 1786. — Height (with lid and dish) 15.0 cms. Privately owned.

286. Bowl (for slops?), round, with foot and square plinth. Two handles in form of osiers entwined with a band (»fasces«). Chased border of laurel leaves; chased radial gadrooning. The bowl is a companion piece to a smaller bowl of the same form (for sugar?), without handles. Made by Andreas Røymand, Copenhagen, 1777. Height 11.5 cms.

Kunstindustrimuseum
(Museum of Applied Art), Oslo.

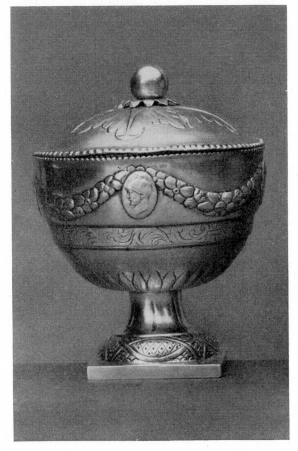

287. Bowl, for sugar or sweets, with lid. Hemispherical, with chased festoons of flowers and medallions with Roman portraits, square plinth and round coussinet foot with chased cross-bands on background of lozenges and scales. Domed lid with bead edging and fruit finial. In the lid is pricked the inscription (here translated) »In Memory of 17th June 1789«. Made by Christian Nielsen Lindbach, Copenhagen, ca. 1789. Height 12 cms.   Danish Museum of Decorative Art.

288. Sugar-bowl, vase-shaped with round coussinet foot and square plinth. The bowl is chased with festoons of drapery and medallions, the under section with pointed radial leaves, the upper rim and coussinet with a lozengy border. Beaded edge. Bow handle. The sugar-bowl, designed along with spoon sifter for use with granulated sugar made its first appearance in the 1770's. Gradually this and other types of sugar-bowls superseded the sugar-dredger. Made by unknown Copenhagen goldsmith 1778. Height (without handle) 12.5 cms.

Municipal Museum of Copenhagen.

289. Sugar-bowl, with lid, vase-shaped, with square plinth. Lightly engraved with leaves around an oval panel with owner's initials and date 1805. Bead edges around foot and upper rim and on the high domed lid. Movable bow handle. Made by Nicolai Brandt, Horsens, ca. 1805. Height (with handle) 24.0 cms.

Danish National Museum.

290. Sugar-bowl, vase-shaped, with vertical slots backed by inset silver liner; handles with scrolls and right-angles. Made by Poul Jensen Theilgaard, Odense (master crafts-man 1792—1820). Height 16.0 cms.   Privately owned.

291. Sugar-bowl, vase-shaped. Filigree work, base resting on balls. Cut crystal glass liner. High pierced side handles. Made by Frederik Moritz Klose, Copenhagen, 1812. Height 19.5 cms.   Privately owned.

292. Sugar-bowl, vase-shaped, on stand. Openwork sides engraved with festoons of drapery and chaplet of leaves. Blue glass liner. Movable bow handle, lightly engraved. Rim with hoops holding twelve tea-spoons. Made by Bendix Gijsen, Copenhagen, 1810. Height (without handle) 15.5 cms.   Privately owned.

293. Sugar-bowl, silver parcel-gilt. Spherical container, the upper half opening like a lid when the finial is depressed. Suspended in a stand with caduceus, masks and festoons on a pillared foot in which are inserted ten tea-spoons. Made by Bendix Gijsen, Copenhagen 1807. Height 34.8 cms.   Privately owned.

294. Sugar-bowl, boat-shaped. The inside is gilt. Border chased with vine leaves and shields. Two lion masks with rings. Four fluted, curved legs with lion feet on stand. Made by unknown Copenhagen goldsmith, 1813. Height 13.0 cms.

Privately owned.

295. Sugar-bowl, boat-shaped, with chased leaf border. Four cast curved legs decorated with mussels and dolphins, terminating in animal heads and resting on plain oval base; in the centre of this is a bird cast on a dome. Engraved with King Frederik VI's crowned monogram. Made by Michael Foght, Copenhagen, 1823. Height 13.0 cms.

Privately owned.

296. Slop-bowl, round, chased with border of vine-leaves and shield cartouches. Made by Halvor Hellesen, Slagelse, 1814. Height 8.8 cms.   Privately owned.

297. Sugar-bowl, with high foot. Two spiral handles. Gadrooned rim. Chased leaf borders; a palmette border around the stem. Made by Nicolai Brandt Lorentzen, Copenhagen, 1832.
          Privately owned.

304. Centre piece (épergne) with bowls (for sweets etc.). Stand consisting of four scrolled legs, resting on black wooden knobs. Four detachable fluted bowls; on the top of the stand a basket with pierced ornaments. Made by Brandt Jonsen, Copenhagen 1779. Height 33.0 cms.   Privately owned.

298. (See opp., top left). Small bowl, oval, fluted, on four curved feet. Made by Jerome Paul Lenoir, Copenhagen, c. 1750—60.   Privately owned.

299. (See opp., top right). Small bowl, shell-shaped, on three curved feet. Upright handle. Made by Jens Sander Schouw, Copenhagen, ca. 1760. Height 5.0 cms.   Privately owned.

300. (See opp., left centre). Sugar-bowl, with foot, oval, fluted. Made by Jens Christensen, Copenhagen, 1740. Height 6.0 cms.   Privately owned.

301. (See opp., right centre). Sugar-bowl, with foot, oval, fluted. Made by Jens Nielsen Randers, Copenhagen, 1731. Height 6.2 cms.   Privately owned.

302. (See opp., bottom left). Sugar-bowl, with foot, oval, fluted with chased rococo ornament. Made by unknown Aabenraa goldsmith, ca. 1760. Height 4.3 cms.   Privately owned.

303. (See opp., bottom right). Sugar-bowl, with foot, oval; engraved flowers on the bottom. Four curved legs resting on base. Made by Nicolai Hansen, Tønder (master crafts-man 1790—1825). Height 5.0 cms.   Privately owned.

305. Pot, with lid, with three straight legs and straight handle. On the lid are three balls, so arranged that the lid can be used as a bowl. Engraved clusters of fruit and landscape with houses, animals and a hunter, and initials showing that the pot was made for Madtz Povelsen, a Mayor of Randers, and his wife Anna Nielsdatter (married in 1621); there are also the names and dates of the successive members of this family who have owned this pot up to the present day (cf. no. 312). Made by Ove Nielsen, Aarhus in the 1620's. Height 15.0 cms. Privately owned.

306. Pot with lid, on three straight legs. Domed lid, with large flower-shaped finial. Side handle terminating in similar finial. Made by Povel Knudsen Lund, Aalborg (master craftsman 1767—94). Height 18.5 cms.   Privately owned.

307. Pot, with twisted fluting, resting on three curved legs. Side handle of black wood with small white bone finial. Made by Rasmus Møller, Odense, 1760—80. Height 10.0 cms.   Privately owned.

308. Pot, with lid, spout, four short legs and projecting bone handle. Chased with leaf festoons; the lid is chased with leaves around a flower-shaped finial. The inside is gilt. Made by Christian Werum, Copenhagen, 1784. Height 11.5 cms.
Privately owned.

309. Bowl, oval, plain, on low moulded foot; leaves and fruit engraved on the sides. One lug-handle in the form of a leaf, the other shaped like a pine-cone. Bowls of this type, generally with one or two flat lug-handles, are called »kovsken« and are used especially as drinking vessels. Made by Gert Hermands, Aalborg (master craftsman 1548—1600). Height 6.7 cms.

Privately owned.

310. Bowl, with lug-handles (»kovsken«), round, with swelling side, engraved with Renaissance ornament. Two flat clover-leaf handles engraved with the owner's initials. Engraved on the side are the same initials and two coats-of-arms belonging to commoners. Made by unknown Naestved goldsmith 1608. Height 6.0 cms.

Danish National Museum.

311. Bowl, with lug-handle (»kovsken«), resting on low moulded foot. The side is lightly engraved with Renaissance ornament and the owner's name. One handle a flat clover-leaf, with flower engraving, the other cast in the shape of a man's figure. Made by Didrich Seede, Kolding (master craftsman 1637—58). Height 7.0 cms.

Privately owned.

312. Bowl, with lug handles, on low moulded foot, engraved with lozengy border. Two flat clover-leaf handles. Lid slightly domed, with three ball feet, arranged so that the lid itself can be used as a bowl. The sides are lightly engraved with Renaissance ornament. On the lid is the date 1594 and the owner's monograms NI and MCD, referring to Niels Jacobsen, a Mayor of Randers, and his first wife; through later inscriptions the ownership of the bowl can be traced in the same family down to the 18th Century. (This family is identical with the owners of No. 305). Made by unknown Danish goldsmith ca. 1594. Height 11.0 cms.   Privately owned.

313. Bowl, of Chinese blue porcelain, in silver mounting. Chased band arabesques on the foot. Foliated rim mounting, with small tongues. Two bow handles with caryatids. Mounting made by Jacob Thor Borch, Copenhagen, 1608. (The hall-mark on the silver mount of this bowl is the earliest known example of the use of three towers as the Copenhagen mark). Height 11.5 cms.   Privately owned.

314. Bowl, with lug-handle (»kov-sken«), round, engraved with Renaissance ornament; flat clover leaf handle engraved with the owner's initials. Buried during the Swedish War of 1658—60 and since unearthed. Made by unknown Danish goldsmith. Height 2.8 cms.   Danish National Museum.

315. Bowl, with lug-handle (»kov-sken«), oval, octagonally gadrooned with a flat handle on which is engraved the owner's name (Lambert Sørensen Rafnsø 1662); the opposite handle is a hook. Made by Hans Olufsen, Vejle, ca. 1662. Height 2.3 cms.

Privately owned.

316. Bowl, with lug-handles, octagonally gadrooned, with two flat handles supported by cast brackets. The side is matted; owner's initials and the date 1672 engraved in a round panel. Made by Hans Thuresen, Aalborg, ca. 1672. Height 6.4 cms.

Privately owned.

317. Bowl, with swelling side, moulded foot and two cast leaf-shaped lug-handles, supported by openwork brackets. Engraved with «auricular« ornament (which seldom appears on silverware — cf. No. 16), together with the owner's initials and the date 1654. Made by Hermand Jensen, Aalborg, ca. 1654. Height 10.0 cms.   Privately owned.

318. Bowl, octagonal, the sides engraved with flowers and fruit; two cast S-shaped handles. The inside is gilt. Made by unknown Danish goldsmith in the second half of the 17th Century. Height (with handle) 8.0 cms.   Privately owned.

319 a—b. Bowl, with lid, oval, gadrooned, with four ball feet. On the lid also are four balls, so arranged that the lid when inverted can be used as a bowl. Two S-shaped handles. Chased flowers; in the lid is engraved the cypher LB, repeated and reversed. Made by Anders Jensen, Odense, approx. 1680—90. Height 13.5 cms.   Privately owned.

320. Bowl, oval, plain, with rim spreading outwards. Two curved, cast handles with animal heads. Four ball feet. On the one side is engraved a cypher, repeated and reversed, on the other an unknown coat-of-arms. Made by Poul Ottesen Kjærulff, Ringkøbing, ca. 1710. Height 12.7 cms.   Privately owned.

321. Bowl with lid, swelling sides, oval, plain. Two cast curved handles with animal heads and masks. Three ball feet. Domed lid with three balls, arranged so that the lid when inverted can be used as bowl. On the lid a wavy acanthus garland is engraved around a cypher, repeated and reversed. Made by Mathias Hielm, Copenhagen, 1687. Height 16 cms.   Kunstindustrimuseum (Museum of Applied Art), Oslo.

322. Bowl, plain, with fluted upper rim; on the side two unknown coats-of-arms are engraved below a crown. Cast handles, decorated with acanthus leaves, supported by fluted rings. Made by Jesper Hansen Rust, Odense, 1699. Height 6.2 cms.   Privately owned.

323. Bowl, with lid, resting on four ball feet. Chased radial gadrooning on the side and rim of the lid; finial in the form of a pine-cone; cast, curved handles with acanthus and eagle heads. The inside is gilt. Made by Jens Pedersen Komløv, Copenhagen, 1716. Height 18 cms.   Privately owned.

324. Bowl, with lid, oval, resting on four ball feet. Chased radial gadrooning on the side and rim of the lid. Plain cartouches on the sides. Finial in the form of a pine-cone. Two cast handles. Made by Morten Christensen Kirchhof, Copenhagen, 1718. Height 17.5 cms. Privately owned.

325. Bowl, with lid, oval. Chased gadrooning on bowl and lid. Two cast handles. Snake handle on the lid. Made by Carl Simon J. Schwartz, Odense, ca. 1715. Height 9 cms. Privately owned.

326. Gilt bowl, with lid; dish to match; round, low, with swelling body. Two drop handles on the body and one on the lid. Engraved strapwork. Made by Ole Flores Wilcken, Copenhagen, 1734. Height 10.6 cms.   Rosenborg.

327. Bowl, with lid and dish. The bowl is round, fluted, with two bow handles. On the lid is a movable handle. Dish with shaped rim. Made by Fridrich Holling, Copenhagen, 1732. Height of the bowl 9.8 cms.   Frederiksborg.

328. Bowl, with lid, round, fluted, three drop handles with black wooden grips. Made by Philip Lorenz Weghorst, Copenhagen, 1733. Height 8.8 cms.   Privately owned.

329. Bowl, with lid, oval, fluted; cast bow handles; on the lid is a flower-shaped finial. Made by Christopher Jonsen, Copenhagen, 1756. Height 12.5 cms.   Privately owned.

330. Bowl, with lid, round, plain, with drop handles; the side engraved at a later date with the coat-of-arms of a Count Wedell. Low domed lid with ball-shaped finial. Made by Copenhagen goldsmith at the beginning of the 18th Century. Height 20 cms.   Privately owned.

331. Soup bowl with lid; fluted, on low moulded foot; cast handles with rococo shells. Domed, stepped, fluted lid with flattened finial. On the side is engraved a crown and cypher, repeated and reversed. The inside is gilt. Made by Tyge Madsen Werum, Copenhagen, 1733. Height 23 cms.   Privately owned.

332. Soup bowl with lid; oval, with curved and fluted sides; cast side-handles with shells. On the lid is a fruit-shaped finial. The inside is gilt. Made by Nicolai Junge, Copenhagen, 1737. Height 23 cms.   Privately owned.

333. Soup bowl with lid and dish, oval, with curved and fluted sides and cast handles. This is one of the oldest specimens of a type of soup bowl that was procured for the Danish Court about 1740; during the next half-century it was repeatedly imitated as additions were made to the Royal Household Silver. All these bowls originally had dishes to match, but only isolated examples have been preserved. This bowl was made by Ole Flores Wilcken, Copenhagen, 1741, the dish by Nicolai Langermann, Copenhagen, 1730. Height 30 cms.

The Royal Household Silver.

334. Tureen, with lid and dish, oval; curved, fluted sides with chased rococo shells. Cast side-handles, foliated; four scroll legs. The dish has a curved, fluted edge with four matted panels containing engraved rococo vines, and in the centre, an engraved view of Our Saviour's Church, Horsens, surrounded by rococo leaves on a matted background. Made by Knud Brandt, Horsens, ca. 1760—70. Height 20 cms.   Privately owned.

335. Tureen, oval, with curved, fluted sides. Cast handles with shells. On the lid is a flower-shaped finial. Engraved cypher SMV repeated and reversed. Made by Jens Olsen Førslev, Copenhagen, 1745. Height 30 cms.

Privately owned.

336. Tureen, oval, plain, with four cast legs; two cast side-handles. Domed lid with large oval finial. Made for the Duke of Augustenborg by Fridrich Christopher Hansen, Aabenraa, (master craftsman 1760—95). Height 26 cms.

Frederiksborg.

337. Small tureen, with lid, oval, with curved fluted sides; three leaf-shaped legs; cast handles with shells. On the lid is a finial in the form of a flower with stalk. Made by Sivert Thorsteinsson, Copenhagen, 1762. Height 12.5 cms.
Privately owned.

338. Tureen with lid, oval, fluted. Four lion feet. Movable bow handles on the lid and (with horn grips) on the tureen. Made by Peter Norman, Randers (master craftsman 1747—61). Height 18.5 cms.
Privately owned.

339. Tureen, oval, plain, with swelling sides, four cast legs and small cast leaf-shaped handles; along the edge are flutings with entwined band (fasces). Plain, domed lid with finial in the shape of a large fruit with leaves. The inside is gilt. Made by Bendix Gijsen, Copenhagen, 1792. Height 30 cms. Privately owned.

340. Tureen with dish, oval, fluted. Four scroll legs and two drop handles with wooden grips. Lid with fruit-shaped finial of black wood. The dish is plain, fluted, with curved rim. Made by Johan Fredrik Schytte, Odense (master craftsman 1795—1824). Height 24 cms. Privately owned.

341. Tureen with salver; oval, plain. Four feet and two handles, cast with rococo shells. High domed lid with engraved and matted radial flutings and fruit-shaped finial. Salver, slightly domed, with curved, moulded edge and line ornament, matted and engraved. The tureen was made by Detleff Pape, Copenhagen 1754, the salver by Christopher Jonsen, Copenhagen 1770. Height of tureen 29 cms.   Privately owned.

342. Tureen with salver. The tureen is round, high, with fluted and swelling sides; on the rim are flutings with entwined band (fasces). Four low, cast, leaf-shaped legs and cast, twisted leaf-shaped handles. The lid is domed, with radial fluting and large cast flower finial with prominent naturalistic leaves. The salver is slightly raised in the centre and has a curved rim with fasces, line ornament, matted and engraved, and the engraved coat-of-arms of J. S. v. Mø-sting, a Prime Minister. In the tureen is a loose silver liner. Made by Johan Georg Høderich, Copenhagen 1777. Height 29 cms.

Privately owned.

343. Tureen with salver. Oval,
vase-shaped. High curved handles.
High domed lid with pine-cone
finial. On the tureen and lid are
chased radial flutings and border
of small circles on a pounced
background. Salver with four
feet, bordered rim as on the
tureen and lid and moulding engraved with leaves in the centre.
The tureen was formerly at
Hvedholm Manor, where there
used to be a similar piece of
French origin. Made by Franciscus Kozlowsky, Copenhagen
1799. Height 44.0 cms.
Frederiksborg.

344. Tureen, oval, vase-shaped;
high foot with octagonal plinth,
fluted. High cast handles with
bead decoration. Domed lid with
pine-cone finial. Chased radial
gadrooning and lightly engraved
borders on the tureen and lid.
Made by Poul Jensen Theilgaard,
Odense, 1798. Height 23.5 cms.
Odense Museum.

345. Tureen with »plateau«; oval, vase-shaped. Cast, foliated handles. Lid slightly domed. Oval »plateau« with engraved leaf border and six feet. The tureen and edge of the lid chased with radial gadrooning; around the rim of the tureen and the finial a leaf-border with palmette decoration. On the tureen and »plateau« are engraved the Royal Danish coat-of-arms, with crown. This piece once belonged to King Christian VIII. Made by Nicolai Christensen, Copenhagen, 1829. Height 44.5 cms.   Frederiksborg.

346. Tureen, oval, plain, with ring-shaped drop handles set in lion masks. Four flat curved legs with lion paws on plinth with ball feet. Lid with handle in form of wavy band. The inside is gilt. Made by Johan Schnee, Copenhagen, 1801. Height 45 cms.
          Privately owned.

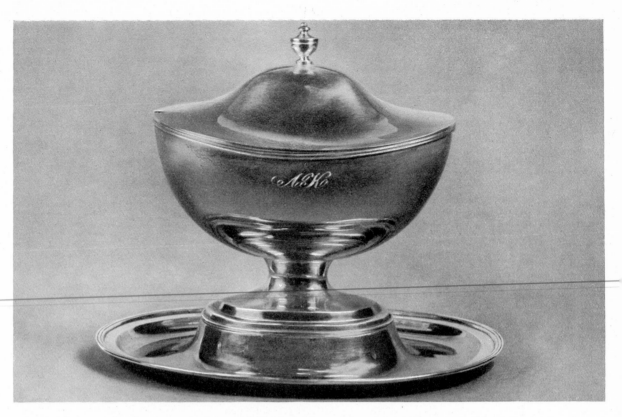

347. Small tureen (for sauce?), oval, plain, with fixed matching dish. Domed lid with vase-shaped finial. The edges of the tureen and the dish are fluted. Engraved initials. One of a pair. Made by Conrad Christian Fredrik Schröder, Copenhagen, 1844. Height 17.3 cms.   Privately owned.

348. Bowl, with lid (for vegetables?), round, plain. Domed lid, large cast flower finial with leaves. The inside is gilt. Made by Johan Georg Høderich, Copenhagen, 1777. Height 17 cms.   Privately owned.

349. Casserole (for vegetables), plain. Domed lid with cast flower finial and leaves. Black detachable wooden handle. The inside is gilt. The casserole, which certainly derives from France, was well adapted for use with a dish-warmer; this is one of the oldest known Danish examples. Made by Christopher Jonsen, Copenhagen 1766. Height 14 cms.

Privately owned.

350. Casserole (for vegetables), plain. High domed lid with large cast flower finial surrounded by leaves. Handle of black wood with white bone finial. The inside is gilt. Made by Johan Georg Høderich, Copenhagen, 1774. Height 16 cms.

Privately owned.

354. Bowl, for vegetables or stews, with lid and plate on dish-warmer. The dish-warmer is bowl-shaped, with base resting on four lion paws and has handles with bone grips. Over the dish-warmer is a flat plate with two small rings set in lugs. On this is a bowl with two plain handles and loose lid. All components have gadrooned edges and palmette leaf borders. On the plate and bowl is engraved the Royal Danish coat-of-arms. The set once belonged to King Christian VIII. Made by Nicolai Christensen, Copenhagen, 1829. Height 30.0 cms.   Frederiksborg.

351. (See opp., above). Casserole (for sauce), round, plain. Low domed lid, with round finial. Black wooden handle. The inside is gilt. Made by Christian N. Hosøe, Copenhagen, 1788. Height 11.0 cms.   Privately owned.

352. (See opp., centre). Casserole (for sauce), round, plain, with spout. Low domed lid, with round finial; black wooden handle. The inside is gilt. Made by Christian N. Hosøe, Copenhagen, ca. 1790. Height 11.0 cms.   Privately owned.

353. (See opp., below). Casserole, low, plain, with lion masks on the sides and small narrow leaf border along the rim. Handle of black wood with white bone finial. Made by Anders Nielsen, Copenhagen, 1806. Height 5.5 cms. Privately owned.

355. Sauce-boat (one of a pair), oval, plain, with shaped and fluted rim and scroll handle. Made by Jens Nielsen Randers, Copenhagen, 1740. Height 11 cms.   Privately owned.

356. Sauce-boat, oval, plain, with fluted rim and scroll handle. Engraved monogram, with crown. Made by Sivert Thorsteinsson, Copenhagen 1742. Height 11.2 cms.   Privately owned.

357. Sauce-boat, oval, fluted, with scroll handle. Made by Sivert Thorsteinsson, Copenhagen, 1742. Height 10.3 cms. Privately owned.

358. Sauce-boat, oval, fluted, with scroll handle. Made by Jørgen Nielsen Lind, Copenhagen, 1744. Height 10.8 cms. Privately owned.

359. Sauce-boat, fluted, on plain oval foot. Two flat scroll side-handles. The type is known to have originated in France in the 1720's. Made by Jens Kieldsen Sommerfeldt, Aalborg, ca. 1750. Height 7.5 cms. Privately owned.

360. Sauce-boat, (one of a pair), fluted, with two scroll side-handles. Plain oval foot with scalloped rim. Made by Sivert Thorsteinsson, Copenhagen, 1750. Height 11.8 cms. Privately owned.

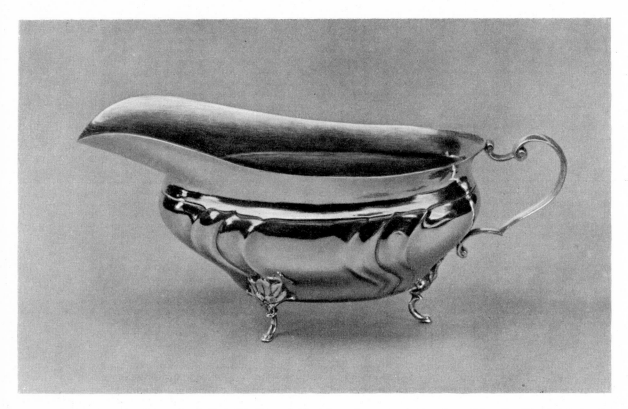

361. Sauce-boat, oval, with twisted fluting, plain raised collar, three cast legs and scroll handle. The inside is gilt. Made by Poul Søren Bay, Copenhagen, 1752. Height 10.5 cms.   Privately owned.

362. Sauce-boat or cream jug, oval, with swelling sides and chased rococo shells, three cast legs shaped like sea-monsters, with rococo shells. Flat bow handle. Made by Andreas Brøndlund, Copenhagen, 1755. Height 6.3 cms. Privately owned.

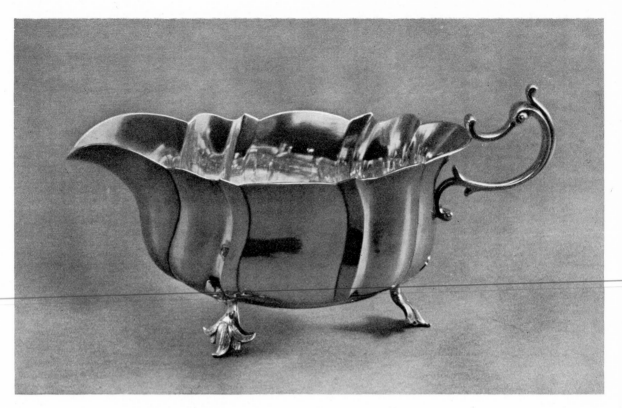

363. Sauce-boat, oval, with swelling sides and twisted fluting. Three leaf-shaped legs and scroll handle. Made by Sivert Thorsteinsson, Copenhagen, 1760. Height 10.2 cms.   Privately owned.

364. Sauce-boat or cream jug, oval, with swelling sides and twisted fluting. Three cast legs and scroll handle. Owners' initials pricked in an engraved cartouche with rococo shells in the side. Made by Jens Nielsen Theilgaard, Fredericia, ca. 1770. Height 7.8 cms.   Privately owned.

365. Sauce-boat, with twisted fluting; plain collar with wavy rim. Three cast foliated legs. Scroll handle. The inside is gilt.
Made by Niels Pihl, Copenhagen, 1780. Height 8.5 cms.   Frederiksborg.

366. Sauce-boat, plain, with swelling sides, oval, with raised open scroll handle, obliquely twisted. In the bottom is engraved Queen Juliane Marie's crowned monogram. The inside is gilt. The design shows French influence. Made by
Jonas H. Jonassen, Copenhagen, 1770. Height 15.5 cms.   The Royal Household Silver.

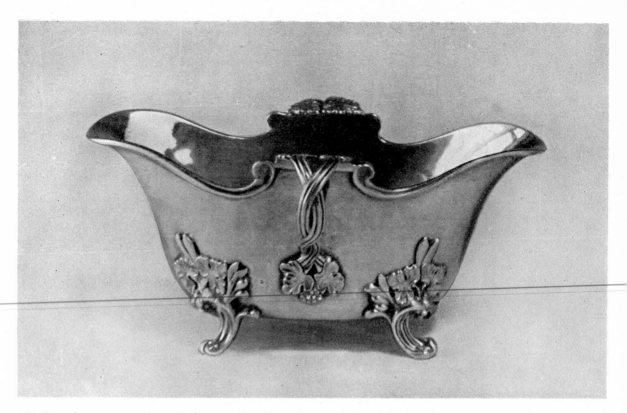

367. Sauce-boat or cream jug with four cast legs. Two plaited and fluted side handles with vine leaves. Made by Sivert Thorsteinsson, Copenhagen, 1774. Height 9.1 cms.   Privately owned.

368. Sauce-boat, small, plain, with cast, fluted edge. Made by Jens Sander Schouw, Copenhagen, ca. 1776. Height 3.4 cms.
Privately owned.

369. Sauce-boat or cream jug, plain, with swelling sides, fluted edge and scroll handle. Made by Johan Georg Høde-rich, Copenhagen, in the 1770's. Height 10.5 cms.   Privately owned.

370. Sauce-boat, oval, plain, with leaf border lightly engraved along the rim. High bow handle. Round foot with square plinth. Made by Halvor Hellesen, Slagelse, 1826. Height 16 cms.   Privately owned.

371. Butter dish in form of an oval tub; flat lid with radially-fluted finial. On the side is engraved an unknown coat-of-arms. The inside is gilt. Made by Hans Jacob Møller, Copenhagen, 1821. Height 10.7 cms.   Privately owned.

372. Dish-warmer; round, pierced bowl-shaped container with loose spirit lamp inside; three scroll legs, terminating in raised bows at the top. Black, turned wooden handle. This piece comes from the Royal Household Silver; the original spirit-lamp has been replaced by one from a dish-warmer of more recent date. The dish-warmer was made by Detleff Pape, Copenhagen, ca. 1750, the spirit-lamp by Christian Hosøe probably in 1783. Height 12.5 cms.   Privately owned.

373. Plate, to which is soldered a moulded rim (now broken off in parts); engraved with a crown and shield containing the three lions of the Royal Danish coat-of-arms. Probably Danish workmanship from towards the end of the 16th Century. Diam. 20 cms.

Rosenborg.

374. Plate, to which is soldered a gilt frieze cast with animals. Engraved with the crown and monogram of King Frederik II (F S = Fredericus Secundus). Probably made by Johan Siibe (died ca. 1564) or Jørgen Jacupssøn (the King's goldsmith 1566—1581), Copenhagen. Diam. 21.5 cms. Rosenborg.

375. Plate with chased birds and fruits on the rim and a rosette in the bottom. Made by Jodocus Henricus Mundt, Copenhagen, 1689. Diam. 17 cms.

Privately owned.

376. Plate, the rim chased with lobed acanthus leaves on a pounced ground. Some of the original gilt still to be seen. Made by Didrich Hoff, Copenhagen, 1701. Diam. 20.3 cms.

Danish National Museum.

377. Plate, the rim chased with acanthus leaves and flowers with two gilt shells. Made by Daniel Schwartzkopf, Copenhagen, 1703. Diam. 23.8 cms. Privately owned.

378. Plate, the rim chased with oblique gadrooning and bead edging, in the centre an engraved cypher, repeated and reversed. Made by Mogens Thommesen Løwenhertz, Horsens, ca. 1700. Diam. 22.2 cms. Privately owned.

379. Plate, with wavy, fluted, moulded edge. Made by Jens Olsen Førslev, Copenhagen, 1741. Diam. 26.2 cms.
Privately owned.

380. Plate, with roped edge. Engraved with the Royal Danish coat-of-arms. Made by Nicolai Christensen, Copenhagen, 1829. Diam. 25 cms.
Frederiksborg.

381. Dish, with wavy, fluted edge. Engraved with crown and the letters C. L., signifying Landgrave Carl of Hesse and Princess Louise of Denmark. Made by Jens Sander Schouw, Copenhagen, 1766. Diam. 43.5 cms.   Frederiksborg.

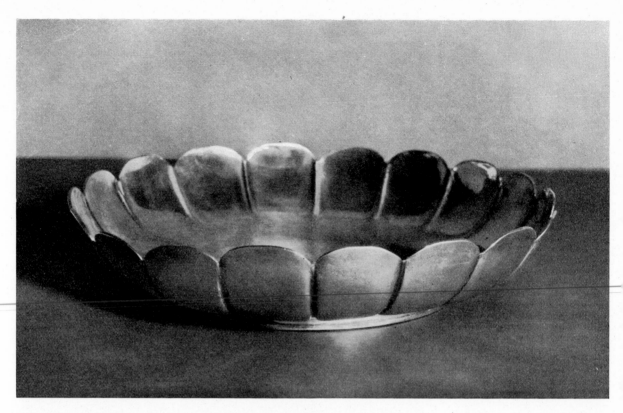

382. Dish or salver, round, with scalloped and gadrooned edge. Made by Mogens Thommesen Løwenhertz, Horsens (master craftsman 1695—1733). Height 3.1 cms. Diam. 16.3 cms. Frederiksborg.

383. Dish, round, plain. Made by Niels Johnsen, Copenhagen, 1722. Height 2 cms. Diam. 14.5 cms. Privately owned.

384. Dish (for tea-pot etc.) with wavy and fluted rim. Made by Johan Jørgen Borring, Copenhagen, 1742. Length 21 cms.
Privately owned.

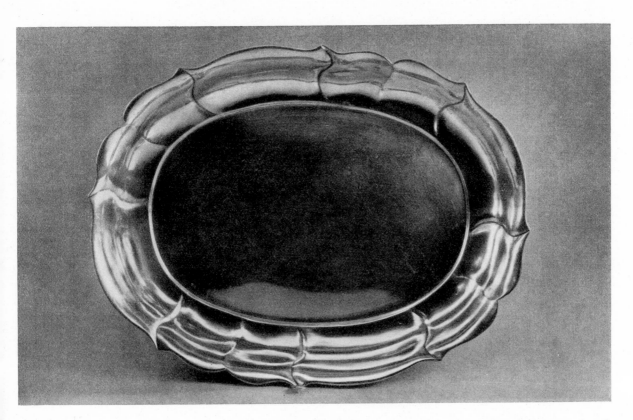

385. Dish (for tea-pot etc.); the rim wavy, with twisted fluting. Made by Jens Sander Schouw, Copenhagen, 1767. Length 27 cms.
Privately owned.

386. Dish (perhaps a tureen salver) with wavy, fluted and moulded edge. Made by Jens Jacobsen Hoff, Copenhagen, 1740. Length 38.4 cms.   Privately owned.

387. Dish (perhaps a tureen salver); the rim is wavy, moulded, with twisted fluting; two cast handles. Made by
Jerome Paul Lenoir, Copenhagen, 1750. Length 45 cms.   Privately owned.

388 a and b. Dish with cover; fluted, with moulded edge. Engraved with Royal Danish coat-of-arms. In the 18th Century dishes were very often used with covers, but later these covers everywhere disappeared. Made by Asmus Fridrich Holling, Copenhagen, 1741—42. Diam. 31 cms.   The Royal Household Silver.

389. Dish, deep, with moulded rim, engraved with the owner's initials and the date 1729. Made by Anders Clausen Schefmand, Aarhus, ca. 1729. Length 42.5 cms.   Privately owned.

390. Dish, with shaped, fluted and moulded edge. Made by Poul Søren Bay, Copenhagen, 1745. Length 47 cms.   Privately owned.

391. Dish with shaped, fluted and moulded edge. Made by Christopher Jonsen, Copenhagen, 1755. Length 49.5 cms.   Privately owned.

392. Dish, with shaped, fluted and moulded edge. On the rim of the dish is engraved the coat-of-arms of the Bille-Brahe-Selby family. Made by Jens Sander Schouw, Copenhagen, 1769. Length 46.5 cms.   Privately owned.

393. Hexagonal dish (for salad) with curved, fluted and moulded edge. Engraved underneath with the crown and monogram of Queen Juliane Marie. Made by Jens Sander Schouw, Copenhagen, 1770. Measurement across 28.3 cms. The Royal Household Silver.

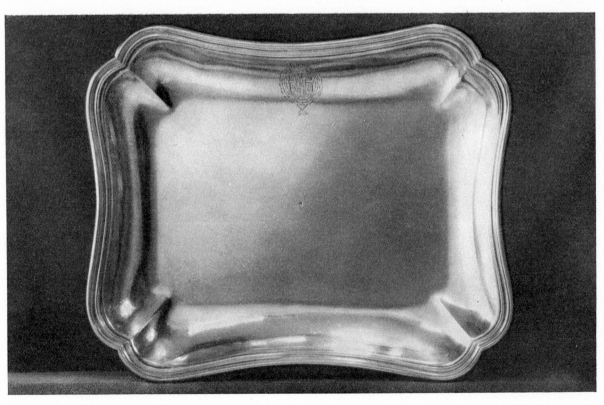

394. Oblong dish (for salad), with in-curved moulded edge. Engraved with the Royal Danish coat-of-arms. Made by Christopher Jonsen, Copenhagen, 1767. Length 29.5 cms. The Royal Household Silver.

395. Salver, with foot, round, with fluted, curved and moulded edge. Fluted foot engraved with the Petersdorff family's coat-of-arms with coronet. Made by Gerhard Hass, Copenhagen, 1758. Height 8 cms.   Privately owned.

396. Salver, with foot, fluted, curved and moulded edge. The foot is lightly engraved with vines; in the middle of the dish is engraved the monogram and crown of Duke Frederik Christian of Schleswig-Holstein-Augustenborg. Made by Matthias Lydersen, Copenhagen, 1796. Height 11.5 cms.   Privately owned.

397. Bread-basket, oval; openwork, with chased medallions and festoons of leaves. Hinged guilloche handle. Made by Thomas Andreas Westrup, Copenhagen, 1792. Height (without handle) 11.5 cms.

Privately owned.

398. Bread-basket, oval, with openwork sides, lightly engraved borders and oval panel with the owner's initials. Hinged fluted handle. Made by Anders Nielsen, Copenhagen, ca. 1800. Height (without handle) 9.4 cms.

Privately owned.

399. Bread-basket, boat-shaped, wire-work. Broad edge with chased border of vine leaves and two shields. Ring handles set in lion masks. Made by Hans Jacob Møller, Copenhagen, 1814. Height 10.8 cms.   Privately owned.

400. Bread-basket, oval, wire-work. Made by unknown Copenhagen goldsmith 1815. Height 7.2 cms.   Privately owned.

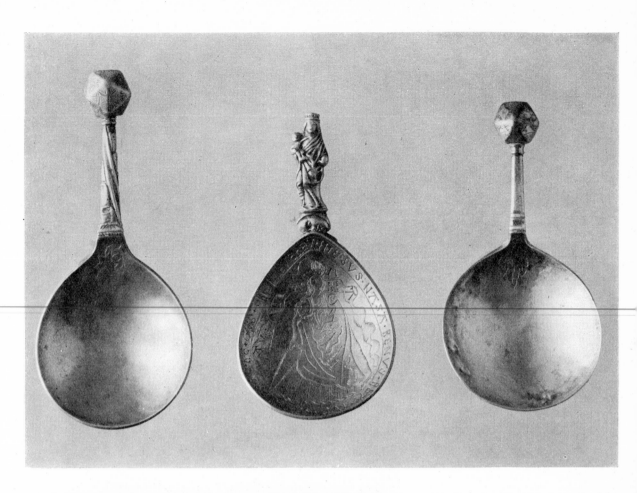

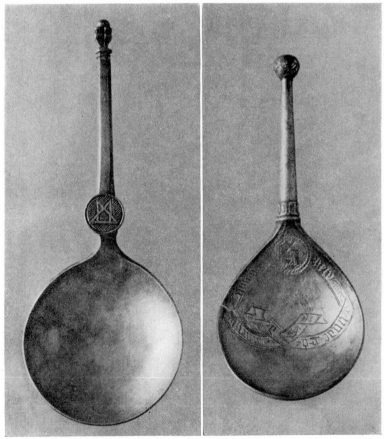

401. Spoon, with twisted stem and facetted finial. Spoons dating from the 16th and 17th Centuries have round or pear-shaped bowls. Older Renaissance spoons are as a rule short-stemmed. Made in Denmark in the first half of 16th C. Length 13.1 cms.

Danish National Museum.

402. Spoon, gilt, with short cast stem in the form of the Virgin and child. In the bowl are engravings. Probably made in Denmark at the beginning of the 16th C. Length 11.5 cms.

Danish National Museum.

403. Spoon with short stem and facetted finial. Probably made in Denmark in the first half of the 16th C. Length 11.5 cms.

Danish National Museum.

404. Spoon, hexagonal stem with gilt finial and round disc ornamented with a star of Zion. Probably made in Denmark about 1350. Length 13.9 cms.

Danish National Museum.

405. Spoon, round stem with ball-shaped finial. On the bowl an engraved inscription. Probably made in Denmark (or North Germany?) in the 15th C. Length 11.7 cms.

Danish National Museum.

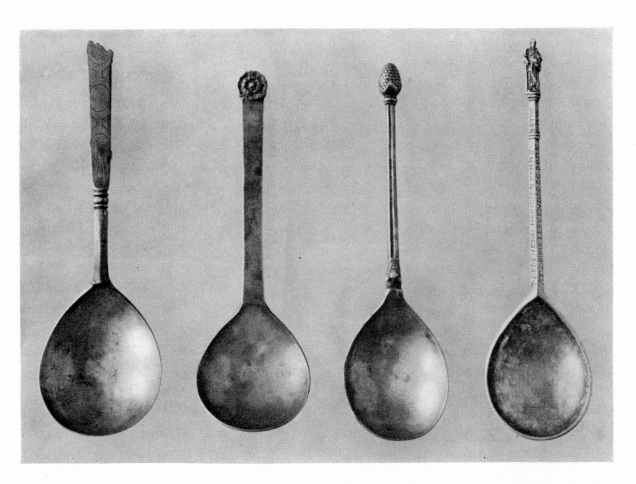

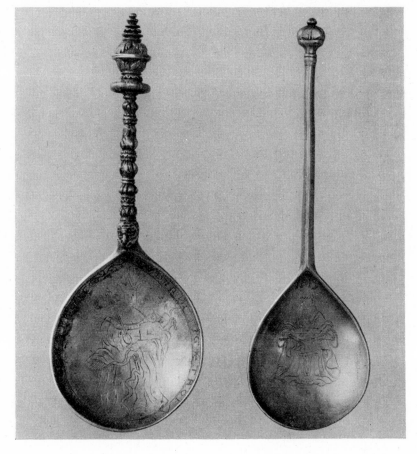

406. Spoon. The outer part of the stem flat, with oblique end and engraved ornaments. Made by Borchart Rollufsen, Copenhagen, 1623. Length 18.5 cms. Danish National Museum.
407. Spoon, with flat stem (cf. No. 423), on the end a flower in relief. On the bowl is engraved the date 1661. Made by Jacob I. Brun, Copenhagen, ca. 1660. Length 16.8 cms. Danish National Museum.
408. Spoon with finial in the form of a pine-cone or cluster of grapes. The so-called »grape spoons« were common in the first half of the 17th C., (»drueskeer«) and survived as a special type until the 18th C. Made by unknown Copenhagen goldsmith 1623. Length 17.5 cms. Danish National Museum.
409. Spoon, thin four-sided stem with figure of an Apostle. Engraved inscriptions. Made by Johan Neue, Copenhagen, ca. 1625. Length 18.5 cms. Danish National Museum.
410. Spoon, gilt. Richly chased stem with acanthus ornament and lion heads. Inscription in Danish. Made ca. 1550—75. Length 14.5 cms. Danish National Museum.
411. See next page.

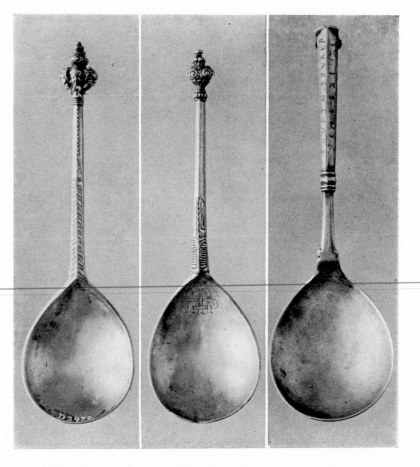

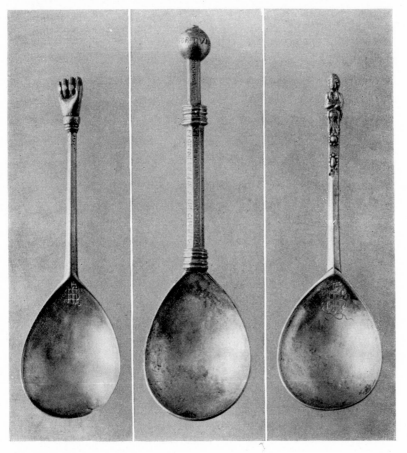

411. (See previous page, bottom right). Gold spoon. Inside the bowl is engraved an IHS monogram and a representation of the Trinity. On the outside are engraved the coat-of-arms and initials of Hans Lykke of Havnø (died 1553) and his wife Johanne Nielsdatter Rotfeld. Probably Danish workmanship about 1550. Length 14.2 cms.
Danish National Museum.

412. Spoon; finial with two cherub-heads. The so-called »cherub spoons« were very common in the 17th Century and are met with in the 18th. Made by Hans Krey, Odense, ca. 1650. Length 16.7 cms.
Danish National Museum.

413. Spoon; finial with scrolls. On the stem is engraved a dragon's head, inside the bowl an IHS. Made by unknown Danish goldsmith in the first half of the 17th Century. Length 16.3 cms.
Danish National Museum.

414. Spoon; Hollow polygonal stem with slipped end crowned by a shield; on the stem is engraved »Søren Søvrersøn 1621«. Made by Mathias Klock Naestved, ca. 1621. Length 17 cms.
Danish National Museum.

415. Spoon with finial in the form of a fist. Engraved with IHS monogram and the owner's initials. Made by unknown Danish goldsmith at the beginning of the 17th Century. Length 16 cms.   Danish National Museum.

416. Spoon, octagonal stem with ball, on which is engraved the word FORTUNA. Latin dedication engraved on the sides of the stem. Made by Didrich Seede, Kolding, ca. 1640. Length 18.5 cms.   Danish National Museum.

417. Spoon; thin stem with male figure. Inside the bowl is engraved an IHS monogram, on the back the owner's initials. Made by unknown goldsmith at the beginning of the 17th Century. Length 15.8 cms.
Danish National Museum.

418. Gold spoon. Finial with scrolls (cf. No. 413). On the back of the bowl are engraved the initials of Queen Sophie of Denmark (née Princess of Mecklenburg) and the Mecklenburg coat-of-arms. Probably Danish workmanship ca. 1600. Length 16 cms.   Rosenborg.

419. Gold spoon. Flat stem. On the bowl are King Christian IV's initials with crown in red enamel. An early example of the flat-stemmed spoon which later came into general use (cf. No. 423). Danish workmanship from about 1630—40. Length 15.5 cms.   Rosenborg.

420. Gold spoon, the back of the bowl fluted. Octagonal stem with King Frederik III's initials with crown in enamel on the end of the stem. Danish workmanship from the middle of the 17th Century. Length 16.2 cms.   Rosenborg.

421. Fork, gold, four-pronged. Flat stem with trifid end, with Queen Sophie Amalie's crowned monogram in enamel. This and Nos. 429 and 430 are the earliest known Danish examples of the trifid stem, which later became characteristic of Baroque spoons and forks. Danish workmanship from the 1660's. Length 18.4 cms.   Rosenborg.

422. Two spoons, flat stems with engraved Renaissance ornaments, cast scrolls and trifid ends. a) The one on the left probably Danish workmanship about 1625. Length 18.4 cms. b) The other made by unknown Danish goldsmith (probably Jens Suenson Suder, Copenhagen) ca. 1625. Length 17.7 cms.   Privately owned.

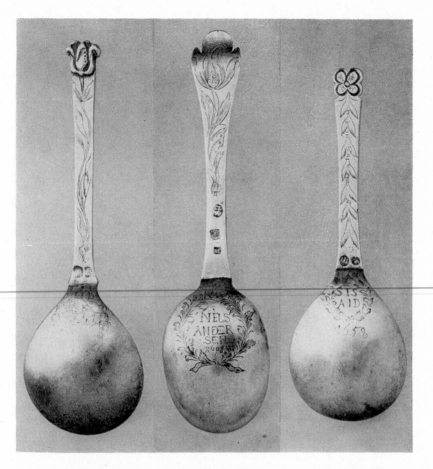

423. Spoon with flat stem engraved with the stalk of a tulip of which the flower is cast and applied. On the back of the bowl is indistinctly engraved a coat-of-arms with owner's initials and date 1656. Spoons with flat stems made their first appearance about the middle of the 17th C. Made by Nicolaus Arenzberg, Copenhagen, 1654. Length 17.5 cms.

    Danish National Museum.

424. Spoon, flat stem with trifid end (cf. No. 421). On the stem is engraved a tulip with stalk, on the back of the bowl a leaf garland with owner's initials and date 1698. Made by Villads Frandsen, Copenhagen, 1698. Length 17.9 cms.   Danish National Museum.

425. Spoon with flat stem terminating in a four-leaf clover. On the stem are engraved leaves, on the back of the bowl a leaf garland with owner's initials and date 1658. Made by Niels Enevoldsen, Copenhagen, 1663. Length 15.7 cms.   Danish National Museum.

426. Spoon, flat stem with flower engraving. On the back of the bowl are engraved the owner's initials. Made by Dionis Willadsen, Naestved (master craftsman ca. 1663—92). Length 17 cms.

    Privately owned.

427. Spoon, flat stem with trifid end, on the back of which is engraved a cypher, repeated and reversed. Bowl with »rat-tail«. This, consisting of a pointed extension of the stem into the bowl (a reminiscence of the days when spoons had bowl of a different material, e. g. agate) became a general feature of Baroque period spoons, probably as a result of English influence. The oval bowl became common from the close of the 17th Century onwards. Made by Lydolph Ridderhus, Aalborg, ca. 1680—1700. Length 18.8 cms.

    Privately owned.

428. Spoon, flat stem with wavy end. Engraved rat-tail on the bowl. Stems with wavy end became common in the first half of the 18th Century. Made by Bendix Aagesen Lund, Copenhagen, 1725. Length 20 cms.   Privately owned.

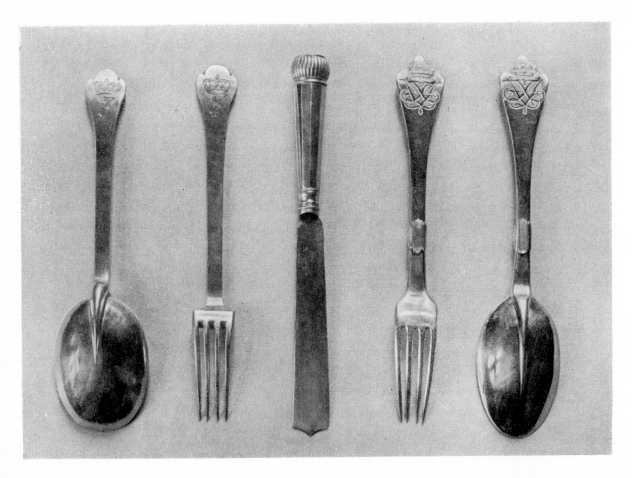

429. Spoon, gold; rat-tail (cf. No. 427); flat stem with trifid end, engraved with King Frederik III's crowned monogram. Made by a Danish goldsmith in the 1660's. Length 18.7 cms. Rosenborg.

430. Fork, four-pronged, companion piece to No. 429. Length 18.4 cms. Rosenborg.

431. Knife with polygonal gold stem, fluted finial with crown and monogram of King Frederik IV in multi-coloured enamel on the finial. Probably made by Fridrich Fabritius, Copenhagen, ca. 1720—30. Length 19.3 cms. Rosenborg.

432. Gold fork, four-pronged; flat folding handle with wavy end; King Frederik IV's crown and monogram in multi-coloured enamel. Probably made by Fridrich Fabritius, Copenhagen, ca. 1720—30. Length 18.7 cms. Rosenborg.

433. Gold spoon, with rat-tail; companion to No. 432. Length 19.6 cms. Rosenborg.

434. Spoon with rat-tail, flat stem with wavy end. On the bowl are engraved the owner's initials and the date 1701. Made by Jesper Hansen Rust, Odense, 1699. Length 19.7 cms. Privately owned.

435. Fork, three-pronged; flat stem with wavy end. Made by Niels Johnsen, Copenhagen 1721. Length 19.5 cms. Privately owned.

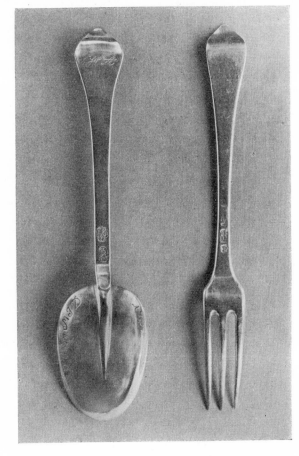

436. Spoon (front and back of the same spoon), flat stem engraved with flowers and stalks and lateral lines. On the back of the bowl is engraved a garland of flowers with the owner's initials and the date 1704. Made by Herman Corditzen Holm, Nakskov, 1699. Length 19.0 cms.   Privately owned.

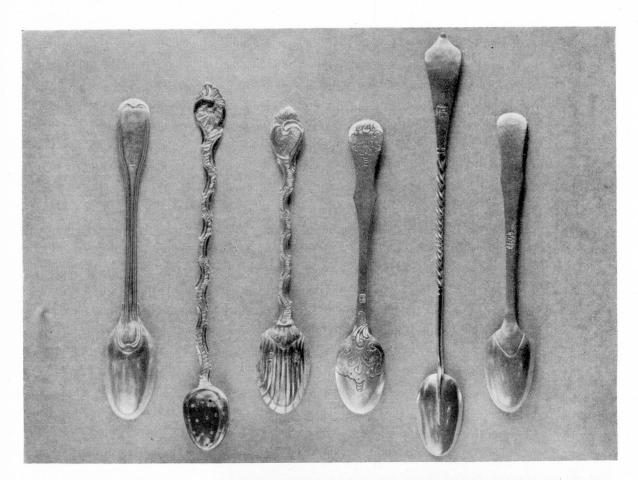

437—444. Tea- and toddy-spoons. Privately owned. — 437. Tea-spoon; handle with threaded edge. Made by Andreas Holm, Copenhagen, ca. 1790. Length 14.0 cms. — 438. Toddy-spoon; cast, wavy stem. The bowl is pierced. Made by A. Schefmand, Aarhus, ca. 1760. Length 16.0 cms. — 439. Tea-spoon with cast, wavy stem; fluted bowl. Made by A. Hansen, Copenhagen, ca. 1770. Length 13.3 cms. — 440. Tea-spoon; flat handle; engraved rococo decoration. Made by Mathias M. Bøegh, Aarhus (master craftsman 1769—90). Length 12.7 cms. — 441. Toddy-spoon with thin, twisted stem. Rat-tail. Made by Peter C. Ove, Copenhagen, ca. 1750. Length 18.3. cms. — 442. Tea-spoon, with flat, plain handle. Made by J. N. Randers, Copenhagen ca. 1750—70. Length 13.0 cms. — 443 a-b. Tea-spoons with flat handles. Engraved rococo decoration. Made by Joachim H. Dysterdijk, Copenhagen, ca. 1760—70. Length 13.0 cms. — 444 a-b. Tea-spoons; handles with threaded edge and leaf ornament. Made by Knud Brandt, Horsens, ca. 1760—70. Length 14.0 cms.

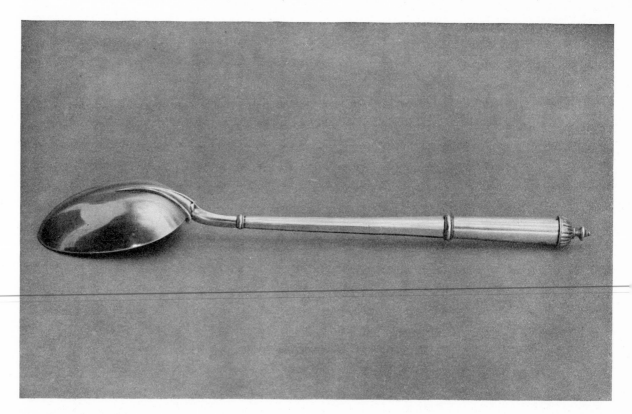

445. Soup spoon with octagonal handle and round end; radially gadrooned finial. Bowl with rat-tail. Made by Jens Christensen, Copenhagen, 1730. Length 41.0 cms.   Privately owned.

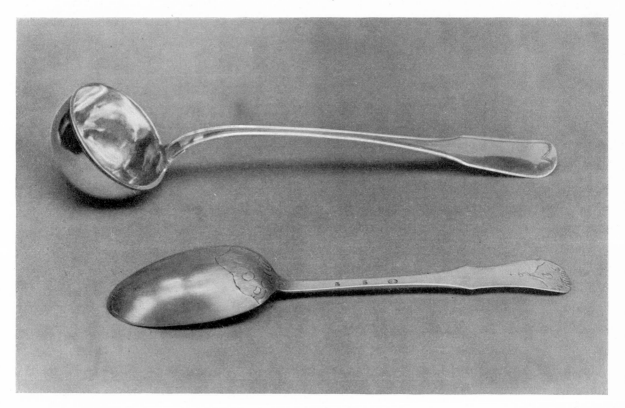

446. Soup ladle, flat handle with threaded edge. Made by Michael Foght, Copenhagen 1791. Length 37.8 cms.
Privately owned.
447. Porridge spoon with flat handle, rococo decoration engraved on the back. Made by Søren Knie, Kalundborg, 1758. Length 32.0 cms.   Privately owned.

448. Dessert spoon, handle with threaded edge and engraved rococo decoration. From about 1750 the end of the handle is usually broad and rounded. Two types of handle are found concurrently, one in the form of a fiddle (e.g. Nos. 448 and 451) and the other in the shape of an oar (e. g. Nos. 449 and 450). At the same time a threaded edge becomes general. Made by unknown Copenhagen master craftsman, 1759. Length 16.7 cms. Privately owned.

449. Dessert spoon, handle with threaded edge and engraved shell. Made by Anders Jørgensen Graff's widow, Copenhagen 1777. Length 16.8 cms. Privately owned.

450. Fork, four-pronged, handle with threaded edge. Made by Jonas Henrich Jonassen, Copenhagen 1768. Length 20.3 cms. Privately owned.

451. Spoon, handle with threaded edge and engraved rococo decoration. Made by Michael M. Foght, Copenhagen 1783. Length 20.8 cms. Privately owned.

452. Spoon with cast, wavy stem; rococo decoration on front and back. Made by Sivert Thorsteinsson, Copenhagen 1769. Length 21.5 cms. Privately owned.

453. Spoon; flat handle; engraved rococo decoration. Made by Andreas Lindberg, Elsinore 1772. Length 21.5 cms. Privately owned.

454. Spoon with flat handle; cast rococo shells. Made by Hans Andreas Toldberg, Copenhagen 1786. Length 21.2 cms. Privately owned.

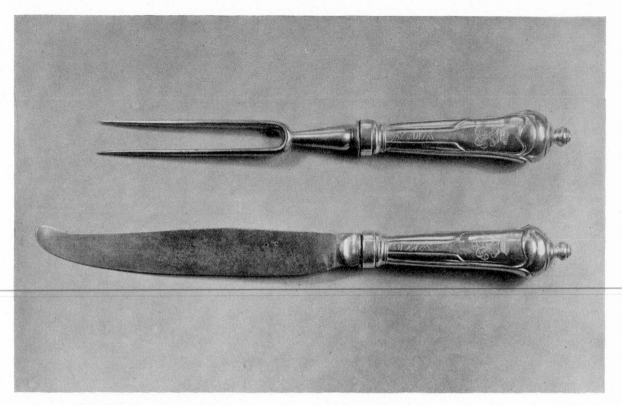

455 a-b. Carving knife and fork with fluted silver handles engraved with the letter K (Knuth) below a coronet; (a) the fork made by Nicolai Langermann, Copenhagen 1757, (b) the knife by Sivert Thorsteinsson, Copenhagen 1745. The two-pronged steel head of the fork and steel blade of the knife are both original. Length of fork 28.5 cms.; length of knife 32.0 cms.   Privately owned.

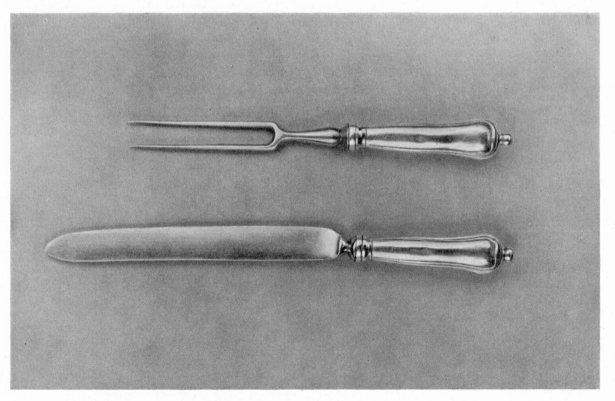

456 a-b. Carving knife and fork, silver handle with threaded edge, on the end of the handle a ball. Made by unknown Copenhagen master craftsman 1758. The two-pronged steel head of the fork and steel blade of the knife are probably original. Length of fork 27.5 cms.; length of knife 34.0 cms.   Privately owned.

457. Travelling set: knife, fork and
spoon in case mounted with leather
and velvet. The spoon and fork have
a flat handle with threaded edge, the
knife a round fluted handle. Owner's
initials engraved later. Made by Johan Jørgen Borring, Copenhagen
174 (4?). Length of spoon 20.5 cms.;
length of fork 18.8 cms.; length of
knife 24.0 cms.   Frederiksborg.

458. Dessert knife and fork with
handles of blue porcelain. Made by
Brandt Jonsen, Copenhagen 1769.
Length of knife 20 cms., fork 18.0
cms.   Privately owned.

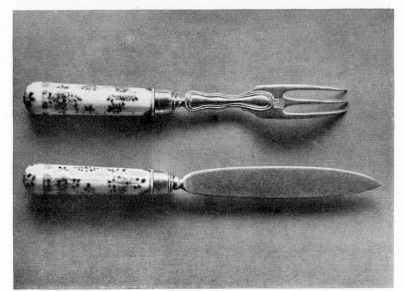

459. Knife with silver pistol handle.
Original steel blade. Made by Johan
Henrich Mundt, Copenhagen 1738.
Length of knife 22.5 cms.
              Privately owned.

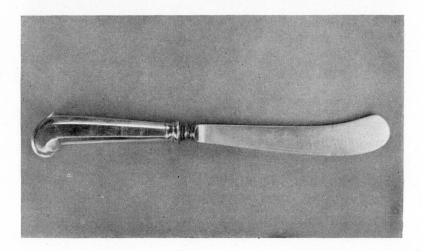

460 a-b. Two forks, four-pronged; the back of the handle engraved with rococo shells, the front plain with engraved initials. Made by Sivert Thorsteinsson, Copenhagen 1772. Length 20.6 cms. Privately owned.

461 a-b. Two spoons, plain handle with rococo shells engraved on the back. Made by Cort Legan Rasmussen, Copenhagen 1785. Length 20.2 cms. Privately owned.

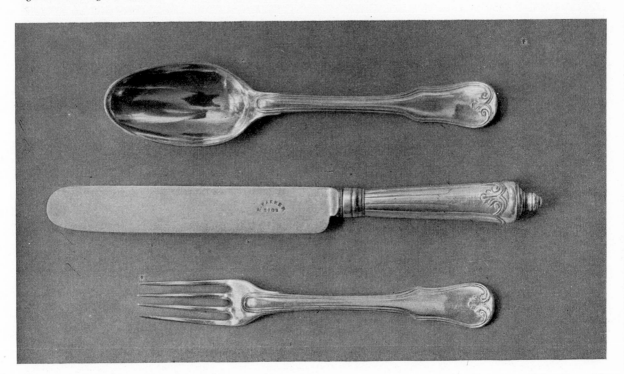

462 b-c-d. Knife, fork and spoon, part of set shown in cabinet on opposite page. Threaded stems and handles with palmettes. Blade of knife is recent, and of steel. Made by Sivert Thorsteinsson, Copenhagen 1753. Length of spoon 20.3 cms.; length of knife 25.8 cms.; length of fork 18.7 cms. Privately owned.

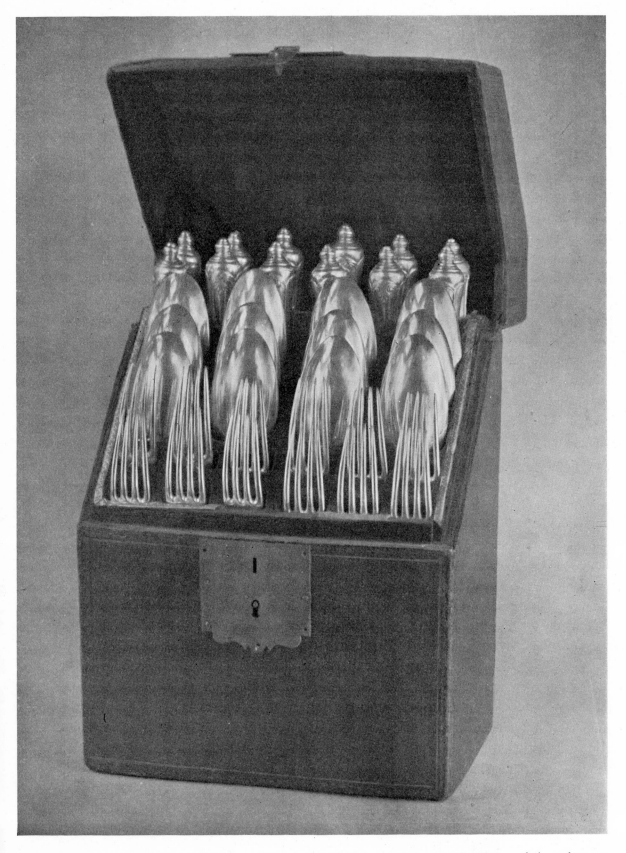

462 a. Cabinet, wood upholstered with leather and mounted with brass, containing 12 silver knives, forks and spoons from 1753 (cf. previous page). Cabinets of this type were quite common in the 18th Century.   Privately owned.

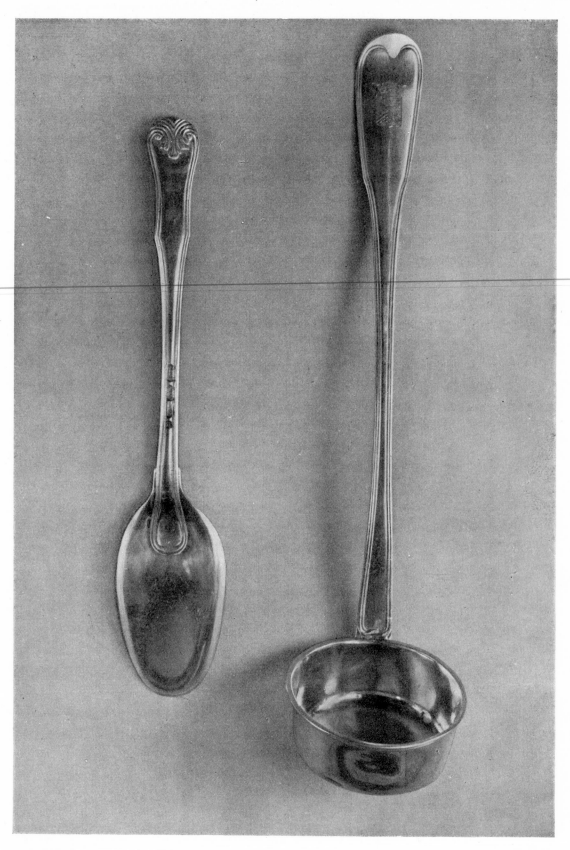

463. Porridge spoon; flat handle with threaded edge and symmetrical leaf ornament. Made by Christopher Jonsen, Copenhagen 1760. Length 30.0 cms.   Privately owned.

464. Soup ladle; handle with threaded edge. On the upper side of the handle are engraved the coat-of-arms and coronet of the Benzon family. Made by Andreas Holm, Copenhagen 1788. Length 37.0 cms.   Privately owned.

465. Porridge spoon; flat handle with threaded edge. Made by Svend Jensen Klitgaard, Copenhagen 1750. Length 31.8 cms. Privately owned.

466. Soup ladle (skull-cap design), flat handle with threaded edge. Made by Svend Jensen Klitgaard, Copenhagen 1754. Length 40.4 cms. Privately owned.

467. Sugar-sifter; flat handle with threaded edge. Sugar-sifters began to appear about the middle of the 18th Century. Made by Jens Jacobsen Hoff, Copenhagen 1753. Length 20.8 cms. Privately owned.

468—70. Three spoons; privately owned. — 468. Flat handle with flower engraving; rounded bowl. On the back is the date 1730. A provincial imitation of an older Baroque form (cf. No. 436). Made by C. Chr. Hoffmeister, Aabenraa ca. 1730. Length 19.5 cms. — 469. Flat handle engraved with flowers. Like the preceding one a late reminiscence of the Baroque. Made by Fr. Chr. Hansen, Ribe (1773—1818). Length 21.8 cms. — 470. Flat handle, cast festoons of leaves and bead moulding. A special neo-classical, South Jutland type. Made by M. P. Hommelhoff, Tønder ca. 1800. Length 21.8 cms.

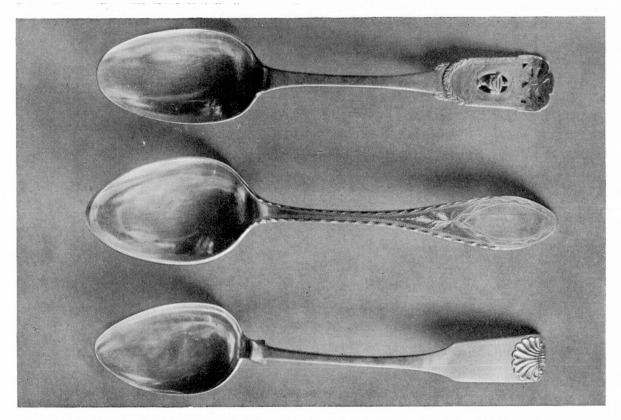

471—73. Three spoons, belonging to the museum at Koldinghus. — 471. Flat handle; openwork bow, festoons and vase. South Jutland type (cf. No. 470). Made by Th. Jensen, Aabenraa ca. 1800. Length 21.8 cms. — 472. Flat pointed handle with engraving. Spoons with slightly pointed bowl and engraved lancet-shaped stem — »Empire spoons« — became common from the 1790's onwards; the type is known in England from ca. 1780 (»Old English«). Made by D. C. Breundle, Aabenraa ca. 1810. Length 22.5 cms. — 473. Flat stem with a cast shell on the handle. »Shell-spoons« with pointed bowl became common from ca. 1830. Made by R. J. Brock, Copenhagen 1837. Length 21.7 cms.

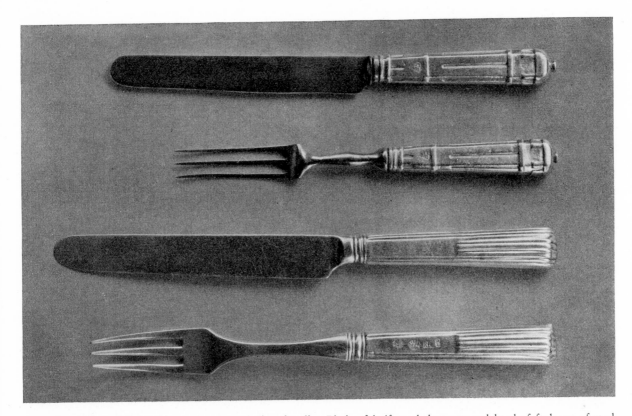

474 a-b. Knife and fork with square, grooved silver handles. Blade of knife and three-pronged head of fork are of steel.
Made by Christian Fridrich Hendrichsen, Copenhagen ca. 1780—1800. Length of knife 17.5 cms.; fork 15.0 cms.

Privately owned.

475 a-b. Knife and fork, silver throughout, with fluted and angulated handles. Made by Rasmus Jørgensen Brock, Copenhagen 1823. Length of knife 19.7 cms., fork 18.2 cms.

Privately owned.

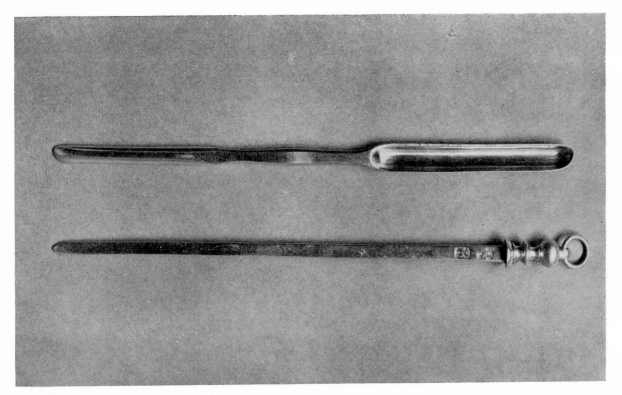

476. Marrow spoon, made by Niels Johnsen, Copenhagen 1724. Length 25.5 cms.

Privately owned.

477. Spit, for game or fowl, with moulded finial and loose ring. Made by Christopher Jonsen, Copenhagen ca. 1747.
Length 25.0 cms.

Privately owned.

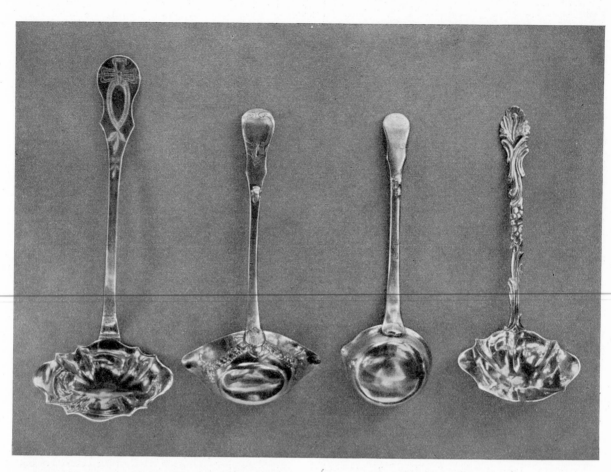

478. Cream ladle; flat handle with engraved bow and leaf garland (cf. No. 471). Boat-shaped, gadrooned bowl, gilt inside. Made by Thomas Jensen, Aabenraa (master craftsman 1796—1825). Length 20.4 cms.   Privately owned.

479. Cream ladle; flat handle with engraved rococo shells and soldered hook. Boat-shaped bowl with chased flower festoons, gilt inside. Made by Michael Foght, Copenhagen ca. 1785. Length 16.1 cms.   Privately owned.

480. Cream ladle; flat plain handle with soldered hook. Round bowl with small spout, gilt inside. Made by Mathias M. Bøegh, Aarhus (master craftsman 1769—90). Length 16.4 cms.
        Privately owned.

481. Cream ladle; cast handle with rococo leaves and flowers; soldered hook. Boat-shaped, gadrooned bowl, gilt inside. Made by Thomas Johan Schorler, Slagelse ca. 1770. Length 16.4 cms.
        Privately owned.

482. Cream ladle; flat handle with engraved rococo shells; soldered hook. Boat-shaped gadrooned bowl, gilt inside. Made by Henrik Wilcken Schorler, Naestved 1785. Length 18.5 cms.
        Privately owned.

483. Cream ladle; flat lancet-shaped handle with delicate Empire engraving (cf. No. 472). Round bowl, gilt inside. Made by Diedrich Christopher Breundle, Aabenraa (master craftsman 1807—22). Length 16.5 cms.   Privately owned.

484. Sugar-sifter (cf. No. 467); flat handle with engraved rococo cartouche containing owner's initials and date 1780, pierced bowl. Made by Jørgen Friis, Randers ca. 1780. Length 21.5 cms.
        Privately owned.

485. Punch ladle; gadrooned bowl with engraved openwork lid; gilt inside. Turned ebony stem with bone finial. A common rococo type. Made by Rasmus Møller, Odense ca. 1775. Length 42.5 cms.   Privately owned.

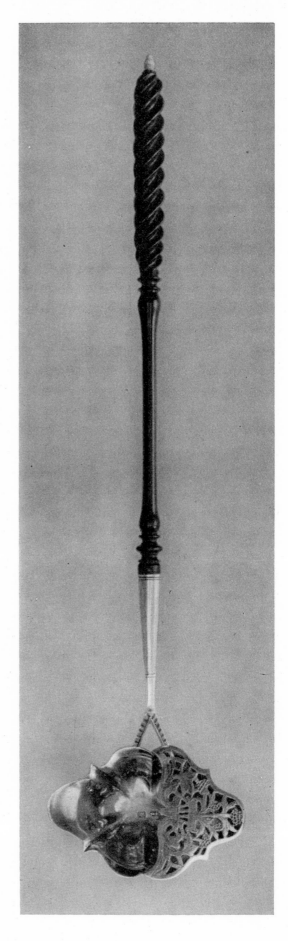

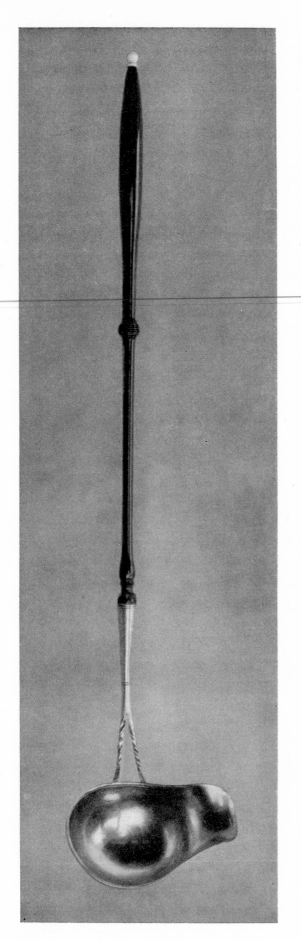

486. Punch ladle; plain bowl with spout. Gilt inside. Turned black wooden handle with bone ball finial. Common Empire type. Made by an unknown goldsmith, Copenhagen in the 1820's. Length 44.5 cms.　　　Museum of Decorative Art, Copenhagen.

487. Fish-slice or cake-spoon with trowel, engraved and pierced. Made by Brandt Jonsen, Copenhagen 1763. Length 28.0 cms.
Privately owned.

488. Fish-slice or cake-spoon, flat handle with threaded edge; leaf-shaped, pierced trowel with engraved neo-classical flowers and stalks and oval cartouche. Made by Johan Georg Høderich, Copenhagen 1779. Length 28.2 cms.　　　Privately owned.

489. Fish-slice or cake-spoon; flat handle with engraved rococo ornament. Pierced, egg-shaped trowel engraved with neo-classical ornaments. Made by Johan Henrich Kemerer, Copenhagen 1783. Length 27.2 cms.　　　Frederiksborg.

490. Fish-slice or cake-spoon with pointed stem and oval, pointed trowel. Engraved Empire ornament. Made by Meyer Nathan Levy, Copenhagen 1805. Length 28.0 cms.
Danish National Museum.

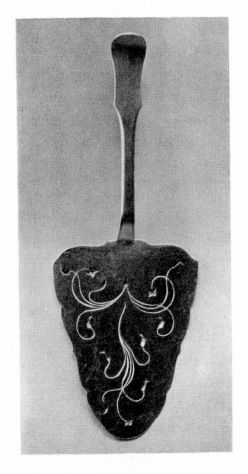

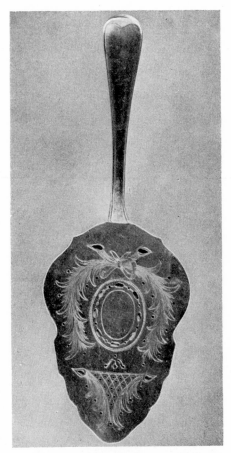

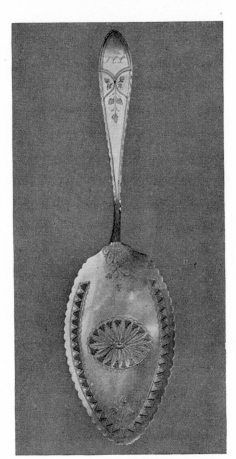

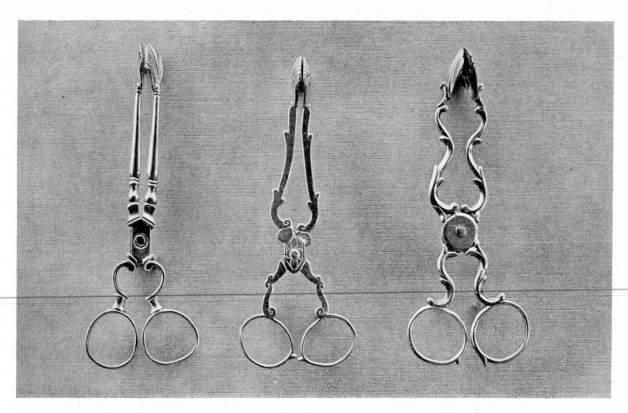

491—93. Sugar-tongs. Privately owned. — 491. Baluster-shaped arms and tongs in the form of shells. Made by Mathias Møller, Copenhagen ca. 1750. Length 12.0 cms. — 492. Curved arms and shell-shaped tongs. Made by Christian Høvring, Randers ca. 1770. Length 11.5 cms. — 493. Curved stalk-shaped arms and shell-shaped tongs. Made by Andreas Holm, Copenhagen 1781. Length 12.0 cms.

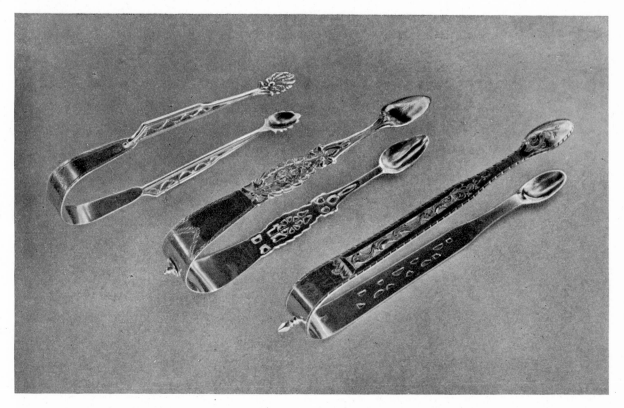

494—96. Sugar-tongs. Privately owned. — 494. Openwork festoons on the arms; shell-shaped tongs. Made by Johan Heinrich Schou, Aabenraa ca. 1800—1810. Length 14.0 cms. — 495. Neo-classical leaf garlands with bows in pierced work on the arms; spoon-shaped tongs. Made by Martin Hinrich Petersen, Haderslev ca. 1790—1800. Length 16.3 cms. — 496. Pierced and engraved leaf ornament on the arms; spoon-shaped tongs. Made by Johan Adolf Müller, Haderslev (master craftsman 1789—1850). Length 17.5 cms.